The life of Pontiac the conspirator, chief of the Ottawas : together with a full account of the celebrated siege of Detroit.

Edward Sylvester Ellis

THE LIFE OF

Chief of the OTTAWAS.
TOGETHER WITH A FULL ACCOUNT OF THE CELEBRATED
SIEGE OF DETROIT

BY EDWARD S. ELLIS,
AUTHOR OF LIVES OF "CROCKETT," "BOONE," "KIT CARSON," ETC.

BEADLE AND COMPANY,
LONDON: 44, PATERNOSTER ROW;
NEW YORK: 141, WILLIAM STREET.

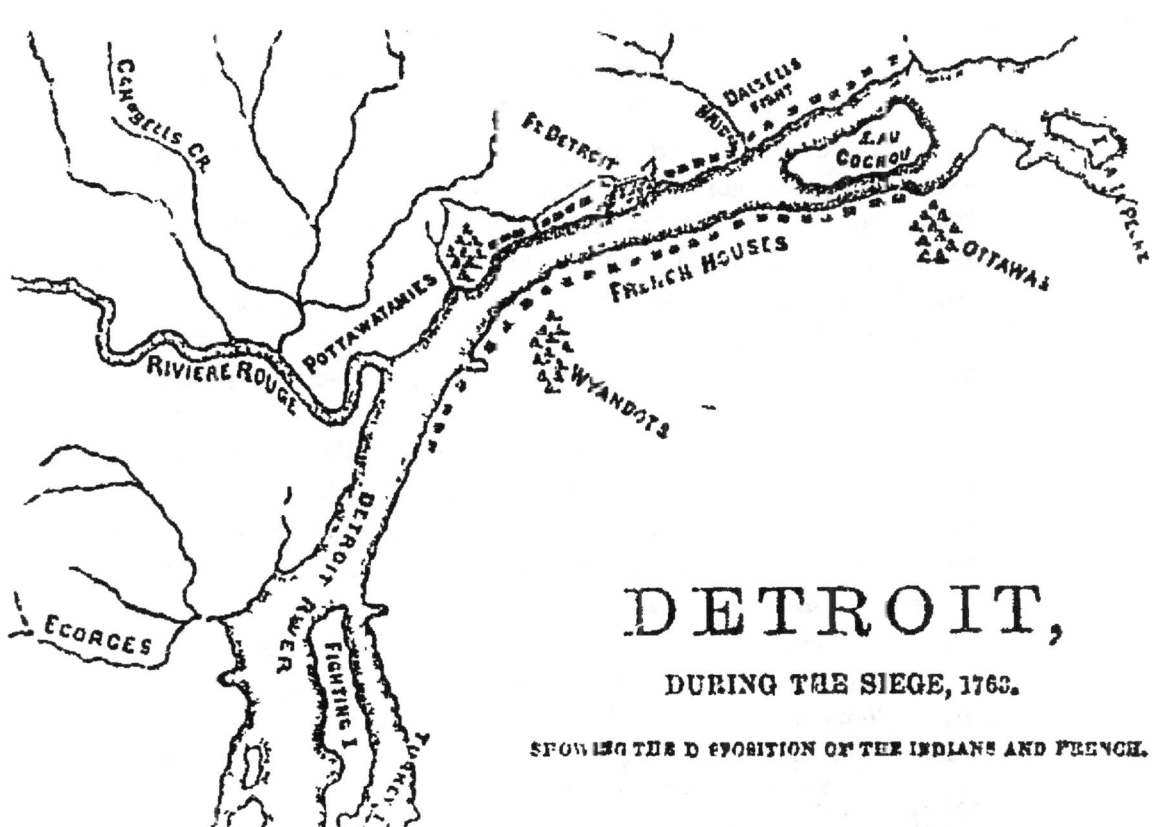

THE LIFE OF PONTIAC.

PRELIMINARY CHAPTER.

A BRIEF ACCOUNT OF THE PRINCIPAL INDIAN TRIBES THAT FORMERLY OCCUPIED THE TERRITORY EAST OF THE MISSISSIPPI

The numerous tribes of North American Indians which, a century since, held possession of the greater part of the territory east of the Mississippi, may be divided into three great tribes or families—the Iroquois, the Algonquin, and the Mobilian. Each of these divisions was characterized by distinct peculiarities in dress, customs and language. The most important were the Iroquois, who, for a time, were absolute monarchs over that vast area inclosed by Quebec and the forests of Maine on the north, and the Carolinas and western prairies on the south and west.* In the north, they conquered the Wyandots, in the east, the Indians of New England, in the west, they uprooted forever the Eries and Andastes, in the south, they "*made Women*" of the Delawares. The confederation as it first existed, included five nations, viz.:—the Mohawks, Oneidas, Cayugas, Onondagas and Senecas. At a later date, the Tuscaroras of the south were added, and, from this circumstance, the name *Six Nations* is derived.† The home of the Iroquois was in central

---

*The different names by which this division is known occasion endless confusion to the student of Indian history. The different English, French and German authorities styled them the Iroquois, Five, and subsequently Six Nations, Confederates, Hodenosaunee, Aquanuscioni, Ongo Honwe, Maquas, Mengwe, Mahsquase, Aggonnonshioni, Palenachendchiesktajeet. The name of Mingoes is applied only to a small branch of the Iroquois which settled near the Ohio. The name Massawomees has been given to several different tribes.

† As a literary curiosity, we subjoin the different names by which the original Five Nations have been known.

MOHAWKS, Anies, Agniers, Agnierrhonons, Sankhicans, Canungas, Mauguawogs, Caneagaonoh.

ONEIDAS, Oneotas, Onoyats, Anoyints, Orneiouts, Oneyyatecaronoh, Onolochrhonons.

ONONDAGAS, Onnontagues, Onondagaonohs.

SENECAS, Slanikes, Chennessies, Genesees, Chenandoanes, Tsonnontouans, Jenontowanos, Nundawaronoh.

New York, where, by means of the vast network of rivers, and the numerous lakes, they were offered the readiest means of penetrating the surrounding wilderness. Add to this their inherent energy, their admirable government, and the true cause of their power is apparent. At the Great Council House in the Onondaga Valley, the embassadors from the different nations were received, and all subjects of importance were there discussed and regulated with the greatest harmony. The system of *totemship* was perfect, and prevented those discords which otherwise would have arisen among the individual tribes. The Iroquois nation, independent of their division into tribes, were separated into eight *totemic clans*, which were bound together by an affection as great as that of the family, and which is preserved among the remnants of these tribes to this day. The members of these clans were not allowed to intermarry, while an insult to an individual was an insult to the whole clan, which every warrior considered it his duty to avenge, as much as if it had been his own particular quarrel.

Another singular custom has been rigidly adhered to by these people—that of descent in the female line. The right of furnishing a sachem being conceded to some particular totemic clan, it follows that the descent of the sachemship must be the same as that of the totem. Thus, if a warrior of the *Turtle* clan married a squaw of the *Hawk* clan, their children were Hawks and not Turtles; and if the warrior were a sachem, the office passed not to his son but to his brother's or sister's son.

In the days of their greatest triumphs, the numerical strength of this confederation was about four thousand warriors; and yet this handful tyrannized over one half of America; their name was as great a terror upon the banks of the far off Mississippi as upon the shore of the Atlantic. While the other tribes were distracted by internal discords, and resolutely abstained from uniting either for offense or defense, their dreaded enemies maintained a perfect harmony among themselves, and kept up a confederation that has never been equaled for influence and strength, by any that ever existed among the aborigines of this continent.

The Hurons or Wyandots occupied the southwestern portion of that peninsula formed by Lakes Huron, St Clair, Erie and Ontario. It is from them that the former lake has derived its name. They spoke a dialect of the Iroquois tongue, and resembled the Five

Nations in many respects. Their number has been estimated at ten thousand; and, although their government resembled that of the Iroquois in many respects, it was not so perfect. Their weakness proved their ruin, for the ferocious Iroquois waged war against them, and in 1649, in the midst of winter, attacked and burnt their largest villages, slaughtered thousands, and scattered the nation forever.

Along the northern shores of Lake Erie dwelt the *Neutral Nation*, so called from its neutrality in the war between the Wyandots and the Five Nations. These were similar to the former in many respects, yet entirely distinct. Their number was about the same and their ruin as complete. Soon after the Huron war, the Senecas managed to pick a quarrel with them, and in a short time they were assailed by the entire confederation, and scattered like chaff before the wind.

This war had scarcely ended, when the Five Nations turned against the Erigas or Eries, dwelling along the southern shore of Lake Erie. In 1655 they were attacked with the greatest fury, and nearly the entire tribe massacred. The remaining members were incorporated with their conquerors or with other tribes, and their name at this day is scarcely mentioned upon the page of history.

The Andastes' villages, dotting the valleys of Upper Ohio and the Alleghany, were next attacked. They were a brave tribe, and maintained the unequal struggle for over twenty years with the most determined courage, but, their doom was sealed. In 1672 they were blotted from the face of the earth by their bloodthirsty conquerors.

Thus, within the space of twenty five years, four powerful tribes were exterminated by the Iroquois, but, unsatisfied with these achievements, they continued in incessant war upon all tribes not members of the confederacy. They drove the Ottawas from the river of that name, in the north, west and south, conquered every tribe that adjoined them, and, at the commencement of the eighteenth century, sounded their war-whoop under the very walls of Quebec.

The Tuscaroras had acted as their allies in their wars upon the southern tribes, and, having suffered a disastrous defeat from the hands of the whites, now applied for admission into the confederacy. They were gladly received, given a seat in the council house, and, from 1715, the name of "Six Nations" becomes applicable to the Tuscaroras.

The members of the great ALGONQUIN division extended from the Hudson Bay on the north, to the Carolinas on the south, and from the Atlantic on the east, to the Mississippi and Lake Winnepeg on the west, inclosing the Iroquois, like an island, in their center. When Jacques Cartier ascended the St. Lawrence, he found the Algonquins along its banks, while Pocahontas, who saved the life of Captain John Smith in Virginia, was the daughter of an Algonquin chief. The savages who made the treaty with William Penn, and the Pequots (or Pequods) who, under Philip and Sassacus, waged war against the New England Puritans, also were members of the Algonquin family.

The Delawares are conceded the first position in this division,* as they claim to be the root from which all other Algonquins have sprung, and the claim is allowed by the other tribes.† It was with their sachems that William Penn formed his celebrated treaty, at a period when they were in the most abject submission to the Iroquois. So complete, indeed, was their subjection, that they had submitted to the name of *Women*, and given up the use of fire arms. Driven further westward by the encroachments of civilization, their ancient spirit returned, and, in the Old French War, they fought against their old enemies on the side of the French. Afterward they declared their independence, and, at the commencement of the Revolution, openly defied their former masters, who soon admitted they were no longer *Women*, but brave and generous warriors.

Probably next in importance to the Lenape are the Shawnees, of whom comparatively little is known. They originally had their home in the south, occupying, it is believed, Georgia and the Floridas. "They were a restless people delighting in wars," and became so obnoxious to their neighbors, that the Cherokees, Creeks and Choctaws combined and drove them from the country. Going northward, they settled upon the Ohio and its branches in the land

---

* The French term the Delawares *the Loup*. They call themselves *Lenni Lenape*, or Original Men.

† The Lenape, on their part, call the other Algonquin tribes Children, Grandchildren, Nephews, or Younger Brothers; but they confess the superiority of the Wyandots and the Five Nations, by yielding them the title of Uncles. They, in return, call the Lenape, Nephews, or, more frequently, Cousins. See Parkman's History.

of the Wyandots, who gladly welcomed them. Here they became a powerful nation, resembling the Iroquois in their demon like ferocity and hatred of the whites.

Along the shores of Lake Michigan, Superior and Huron dwelt the Ojibwas, Ottawas and Pottawatomies, west of Lake Michigan were the Sacs, Foxes and Menomones, and further northward the wandering bands of Knisteneaux.

The Ojibwas, Ottawas and Pottawatomies formed a sort of confederation, and were the first to offer an effectual check to the ambition of the Six Nations. At the mouth of Lake Superior, it is stated, a war-party of the latter were completely routed and almost entirely slaughtered. The fugitive Wyandots and many others found a safe refuge and protection among them.

The MOBILIAN family comprehended the Creeks, Choctaws and Chickesaws of the south. They resembled the Iroquois in many respects, but, as they were far removed from the scene of events described in these pages, and took no part in them, they will not be referred to again in the course of our narration.

THE FRENCH AND ENGLISH COLONIES IN AMERICA

A careful study of the acts of England and France in America is necessary, to understand not only Pontiac's conspiracy, but the causes of the numerous wars which, a century since, raged along the frontier, and opened the way for the Revolution of the colonies. Each nation pursued a different policy. The French settlements in Canada were nursed by the Church and State, and their strength matured under the most favorable auspices; still, they languished and declined, year after year. The outcast colonies of England, forsaken by Government, grew and strengthened like young giants, and soon proved themselves possessed of power and resources that made the mother country glad to claim them as her own. The world can not afford stronger contrasts than that shown in the submissive, priest ridden Canadians, and the stern, vigorous, unyielding Puritans of New England. Champlain, the founder of Quebec, brought four Franciscan Monks from France to assist in the conversion of Canada. Indeed, the sole object of settling the country seemed to be that of gaining proselytes. The priest and soldier, the cross and *fleur de lis*, went together, and the French missionaries, fired by a holy zeal, braved death and torture among the savages. Jean de Brebeuf and Gabriel Lallemant suffered the most horrible death at the hands of the Iroquois. Isaac Jaques and many others were tomahawked, and everywhere the faithful emmissaries were persecuted. Numerous Indians were baptized, and their conversions reported, but their labors were thrown away upon the stolid savages As Le Clercq remarks, an Indian would be baptized ten times a day for a pint of whisky, and, with all the gaudy trinkets of religion upon his person, he was probably a greater heathen at heart than ever

Meanwhile, the French prosecuted their explorations in America In 1679, Robert Cavalier de la Salle passed through Lake Erie in a vessel, through Detroit River, across Lake Huron, and, in birch canoes, coasted along the shores of Lake Michigan, reaching its southern extremity in the month of October. Crossing overland to St. Joseph, he established a fort, and pushed on toward the Illinois wilderness Here dangers began to thicken, his men mutinied, and the vessel, sent back to Canada for supplies, foundered in one of the lakes. Nothing daunted, he left his men in charge of the fort on Illinois River, and turned his face toward Canada He journeyed over a thousand miles on foot through the "frozen forest, crossing rivers, toiling through snow drifts, wading ice-encumbered swamps, sustaining life by the fruits of the chase, and threatened day and night by lurking enemies" Reaching Canada, he found a great cry had been raised against him by his enemies, who had seized upon his property and given out that he was dead He had a warm friend, however, in Count Frontenac, the Governor, and, with another supply of men and provisions, again set out for Illinois The fort he found empty, the men having fled to escape the menaced dangers

The second time the brave man returned to Canada, and, assisted by the Governor, collected means to prosecute his cherished journey With a small flotilla of canoes, he left the fort at the outlet of Lake Ontario and made his tedious way over the surface of the vast inland seas, and finally crossed the portage at the waters of the Illinois His memorable descent of the mighty Mississippi was made, and, on the 9th of April, 1682, he took formal possession of the great valley in the name of Louis, King of France and Navarre

La Salle now visited France, where he was well received at court, and furnished with a squadron of vessels and every means for establishing a colony But the expedition made a miserable failure. The squadron missed the mouth of the Mississippi, the naval commander deserted, and La Salle, with a few wretched followers, landed on the Texan coast Here, while devoting all his energies to the well being of his men, a conspiracy was formed and he was basely murdered.

France, fully sensible of the great advantage of establishing her dominion over this territory, dispatched Lemoine d'Iberville in 1699, who planted the colony of Louisiana. This settlement steadily increased in strength and prosperity, in spite of the wretched manner in which it was governed, and the bursting of the memorable "Mississippi bubble" It was not long before it took rank as one of the most important settlements of France

Canada and Louisiana, being in the possession of the French, they held, as it were, the two ends of the country east of the Mississippi It only remained for her to connect these two extremities. This was determined upon, and at the opening of the eighteenth century the commencement was made Her plan was to establish a series of forts and settlements through the wilderness between the valleys of the St Lawrence and the Mississippi, and thus gain a firm foothold west of the Alleganies, before the tide of English civilization had reached its eastern slope This policy was effectually carried out The fort at the strait of Niagara controlled the entrance to the interior, another at Detroit commanded the passage from Lake Erie, and a third at St Mary guarded the access to Lake Superior The post at Mackinaw held the entrance to Lake Michigan, and those at Green Bay and St Joseph the two routes to the Mississippi There were others at Kaskaskia, Cahokia, and at long intervals the stockade forts peeped forth from the abundant vegetation along the banks of the Mississippi, as far down as Natchez, where the cabins of the Louisiana settlers began to show themselves.

In 1748, Count Galissonniere proposed to France that ten thousand peasants be planted in the Ohio valley, and along the borders of the different lakes But, while this and similar schemes were debating, England was moving forward slowly but surely in the western forests Already the crashing of her woodmen's axes were heard in the Mohawk valley, while scores of cabins dotted the eastern slope of the Alleganies The two great powers that had been rivals for centuries were gradually closing in upon each other, and the hour of collision was rapidly approaching. In one respect France had much the advantage of England. Her widely-separated posts gave her an extended acquaintance with the Indian tribes, and the fur trade of Canada made multitudes of the savages dependent upon her. The St. Lawrence, and the chain of Great Lakes, offered the most extraordinary means of intercourse with the interior, and she neglected no means to propitiate her heathen brethren. Nature had done all in her power, but, south of Lake Ontario dwelt the Iroquois, her implacable enemies. These savages kept up a most incessant war upon her trading companies, soldiers and missionaries, and spread woe in many of her settlements. As early as 1609, Champlain was attacked by a large party upon the river which bears his name. One of the most bloody and merciless wars was thus commenced. The routes between Quebec and Montreal were watched with a lynx-eyed vigilance, and the wretched inhabitants were driven again and again within the palisades and forced to see their harvest fields swept by fire. The fur trade was broken up, and barbarities, too revolting to be described, were perpetrated upon the Canadians. It was not until 1696 that the wisdom of Count Frontenac checked this dreadful butchery.

In 1726, a permanent military post was erected at the pass of Niagara, within the territory of the Iroquois confederacy, and the fur trade resumed with greater vigor than ever. The rapid increase of the French colonies convinced the Five Nations that all opposition was useless. They, therefore, sullenly submitted, for the time, to the encroachments upon their hunting-grounds.

In 1738, La Verandrye established a trading post upon Lake Assinniboine, which was connected by a regular line with those further east, and, with the exception of the Iroquois, was on the best of terms with the surrounding savages.

With the English, the case was different. They now resembled a peninsula, encompassed on the north, west and south by the French. The Iroquois befriended and assisted them in their efforts to establish the fur trade. Many years before (1669) the Hudson Bay Company had been formed, and a fort established at the head of James's Bay. This company prospered greatly; but the scene of their labors was so far to the northward that it is hardly included in the account of the English settlements in America. In 1687, Major McGregory made his way, with a boat-load of goods, to Lake Huron, where he was immediately seized and imprisoned by a party of French. This checked the English fur trade in this direction until 1725, when a post was established at the mouth of the Oswego, on Lake Ontario, where a brisk trade was at once opened with the surrounding tribes. A few years later the Alleganies were crossed by the English traders, to the great disgust of the Governor of Canada, who imprisoned several that were found near the Ohio.

Had the English colonies pursued a policy toward the Indians that common sense dictated, the historian would not be compelled to record the numerous disasters which fell to their lot. In the province of New York they found the powerful Iroquois who bore a deadly hatred to the French, and were naturally friendly to the English. It was solely the fault of the latter that this friendship, a few years later, was forever lost. At the critical period, the Assembly of New York was found to be composed of little-minded men, who considered their own personal interest of more value than the welfare of the province. They quarreled among themselves continually, and the annual present sent by England to the Iroquois was often stolen by corrupt Governors or their favorites.* The negotiations were conducted through the fur and whisky traders, who were literally abominated by the savages. The sagacious chiefs were not long in seeing how lightly they were held, and how differently they were treated by the French.

Not New York alone, but all the English colonies treated the Indians more or less in the same manner. A fatal short-sightedness seemed to have taken possession of them all. Even when threatenings of discontent reached their ears, they failed to take warning; but continued their reckless policy, estranging the Indians more and more, and placing the match to the powder-mine which lay beneath their feet.

France, on the contrary, neglected no means of conciliating her enemies. She treated the chiefs with the greatest consideration, had her agents in every village, flattering them and instilling their minds with prejudice against the English, and carefully abstained from doing any thing that could offend them in the least. Numerous and costly presents were made, and a visit by their sachems announced by the firing of cannon and beating of drums. It is even stated, with good authority, that Count Frontenac, Governor

* Smith's History, New York.

of Canada, plumed and painted himself and danced the war dance with the pleased savages. Further than this did the French go to please their Indian allies. In 1695, the French commandant at Mackinaw most brutally tortured an Iroquois embassador to death, and one of the darkest stains upon the history of France is the inhuman abandonment by Montcalm of the defenders of Oswego and William Henry to an infuriated band of Indians. Hundreds and thousands of the French amalgamated with the savages, and the *coureurs des bois* were in reality as much Indians as though born and nourished in their wigwams. In this manner it may be said that the French became identified with the tribes and the two almost one people.

No such mingling of races occurred upon the part of the English Their traders and *voyageurs* became savages enough in disposition, but an uncontrollable disgust prevented them from uniting their blood with the dusky denizens of the forest. They looked upon them much as we would upon a race of monkeys — a sort of necessary evil which we ever desire to keep at a respectable distance. The remonstrances of the Indians, at the encroachments of the settlers, were met by curses and kicks or a contemptuous silence Their friendship was not esteemed worth seeking, nor their enmity worth avoiding.

One great exception to this manner of settling a country is well known — the founding of the Pennsylvania colony by William Penn, but, as remarked by Mr. Parkman, our admiration of the alleged results of this treaty is much diminished by closely viewing the circumstances of the case. The treaty was made with the Delawares, who, at that time, bore the name of *Women*, and were debarred the use of fire arms. They were far removed from the warlike Iroquois and the tribes of New England, and the very principles of the Quaker faith necessitated a kind of conciliating course toward the Indian When war at length burst forth along the frontier, this philanthropy became a fiery fanaticism The Quakers refused to believe the Indians could ever do any thing wrong, and, even when the German and Irish settlers were massacred by hundreds, and droves of terror stricken inhabitants were flying across the Susquehanna, the Philadelphia Quakers bitterly opposed an offensive war against the savages *

* In 1764, a number of party tracts were published by these men in which they denounced all the whites, who engaged in the war against the

Among the other acts of the English colonies that hastened on the outbreak of the Indians, was the celebrated *walking purchase*—one of the most infamous swindles of the time. In 1737, an old, musty, dingy, worm-eaten deed was brought forth, bearing date far back in the previous century. Its force, if any, had long been destroyed; nevertheless, on the strength of it, the proprietors laid claim to a large tract of land lying on the Delaware. Its western boundary was given by a line drawn from a certain point on Neshaminey creek, in a north westerly direction, *as far as a man could walk in a day and a half*. From the extremity of this walk, the northern boundary was defined by a line drawn eastward to the Delaware river. The proprietors put the most active of the settlers into a vigorous training, cleared a long way for them, and, by this means, made the north-western boundary of an extraordinary length. Then, instead of running eastward in a direct line to the Delaware (as the deed clearly specified), they inclined far to the northward, thus securing an immense and valuable tract of land by the most barefaced cheatery. This *walking purchase* was in the Forks of the Delaware above Easton, and was occupied by a powerful branch of the Delawares, who were ordered to abandon the land at once. Their indignation was so great that they refused to move, when the Quaker Legislature found that force was necessary. This, of course, they themselves could not exercise. Accordingly they summoned the Iroquois, the masters of the Lenni Lenape. These tyrants soon humbled the down-trodden Delawares.

Encouraged by this submission, the English made bolder advances than ever. Numerous families of Germans and Irish crossed the Susquehanna and built their cabins in the valley of the Juniata. The Delawares remonstrated again and again, and finally the Iroquois themselves became enraged and demanded redress for these audacious intrusions. A feeble attempt was made to satisfy them, but it amounted to nothing. The Shawnees and a portion of the Delawares moved westward on the waters of the Allegany and the Muskingum.

Such treatment as this could but alienate the different tribes from the English. The crafty French at this time were penetrating the Ohio valley, and they found the savages well prepared to receive

Indians, in the bitterest terms. While we gladly yield these men all credit for their Christian belief and actions, we can but deplore the blind prejudice displayed in taking the course mentioned.

their insinuations against the English. The friendship of the Iroquois, also, had become colder and colder. In the war of 1715, their indifferent aid gave the English colonies good reason to fear their final estrangement. The French, using every measure to gain and retain the good-will of the different tribes, pressed further and further into the wilderness, until (1753) Governor Dinwiddie, of Virginia, was startled to hear that a body of their troops had crossed Lake Erie and were then on the northern branches of the Ohio. A message was sent requiring their removal. The bearer of that order was George Washington, then but twenty-one years of age.

The results of this mission are well known. The French refused compliance, and the Old French and Indian War was shortly commenced. In 1754, delegates from the different provinces met at Albany, when it was that the plan of uniting their different provinces for mutual protection was first broached. Curiously enough, this policy was rejected by the Crown, as giving too much power to the people, and by the people themselves as giving too much power to the Crown. A treaty, however, was made with the Iroquois, who coldly entered into an alliance of friendship.*

In 1755, the capture of the two French ships, the *Lys* and the *Alcide*, off the banks of Newfoundland, by the English Admiral, Boscawen, closed the doors of peace. The French withdrew their embassador from the court of London, and the war was opened.

It is not our purpose to refer at length to this war. We have only endeavored to show the reasons why the Indians in such numbers were found arrayed upon the side of the French, and why, a few years later, the former friends of the English proved their most implacable enemies. On the 9th of July, 1755, occurred the disastrous defeat of General Braddock. The shameful behavior of the British upon the occasion inspired the Indians with such contempt for them that all wavering and neutral tribes immediately joined the French. In this memorable battle the subject of these pages, Pontiac, led the Ottawas. It is said he then displayed an ability that gave evidence of the subsequent greatness of his life. This is the first mention made of him by history.

Events now follow each other in rapid succession. The battle of

---

* During this council, an Iroquois chief upbraided the English for their invasion of their lands, and neglect of the Indians, adding significantly that the French had treated them like men and warriors.

Lake George, the siege and capture of Louisburg, the successful assault of Fort du Quesne, the route of Lord Abercrombie's magnificent army, the massacre of the defenders of Fort William Henry, and finally the brilliant taking of Quebec—all are comprehended in the space of a few years. The well-tried valor of old England again humbled the pride of France. On the 10th of February, 1763, a treaty was signed at Paris, by which the Government of the latter surrendered to Great Britain all her possessions in North America, eastward of the Mississippi river, from its source to the river Iberville, and thence, through Lakes Maurepas and Pontchartrain, to the Gulf of Mexico.*

It now only remained to take possession of the western outposts where the flag of France still floated in the breeze. The cross of St. George was raised over the walls of Quebec, and the plains around Montreal were covered with her conquerors, but the French still remained at Detroit, Mackinaw, and several important stations. In September, 1760, Major Robert Rogers, leader of the celebrated "Roger Rangers," received orders from Sir Jeffrey Amherst to take possession of the two forts mentioned, in the name of his Britannic Majesty. This, it will be observed, was several years previous to the signing of the treaty in Paris, but Canada had already surrendered, and these forts were included in the capitulation.

At the head of two hundred rangers, Rogers left Montreal, on the 13th of September, in fifteen whale boats. Passing through Lake Ontario, and carrying their boats over the portage of Fort Niagara, they encamped, on the 7th of November, at the mouth of Cuyahoga river, where Cleveland now stands. The weather was cold and rainy, and Rogers resolved to rest his men before proceeding further. Shortly after he had encamped, he was visited by several chiefs, who announced themselves as embassadors from Pontiac. They claimed that country, and, in the name of their great chief, forbade the British to proceed any further without his permission. In the afternoon, Pontiac himself made his appearance, and demanded of Rogers the reason why he had dared to enter his country. The ranger replied that Canada had surrendered, and he was on his way to take possession of Detroit, and restore peace to

---

* Iberville is an outlet of the Mississippi fourteen miles below Baton Rouge, and connects with the Amite river which flows into Lake Maurepas. It now receives water from the Mississippi only at high flood.

all alike Pontiac listened to his words with attention, and, forbidding him to move any further until they had conversed again, withdrew to his own camp and spent the night with his chiefs. In the morning, he replied to Rogers that he was willing to live at peace with the English so long as they were treated with consideration and respect. The officers and chiefs smoked the calumet of peace together, and good-will seemed established upon both sides.

It may seem strange that Pontiac, who, up to this time, had been the firm friend of the French, should form such a treaty with the English; but the far-seeing mind of the chieftain himself affords the true solution of the singular act. The events that had been going on around him for the last few years, showed him that the French power was on the decline, and that self-interest demanded he should make allies of the most powerful. He vainly believed, too, that the English would treat him with great deference, and aid him in his ambitious projects of subduing the surrounding tribes.

Reaching the western extremity of Lake Erie, Rogers received intelligence that a band of four hundred Detroit Indians were lying in ambush at the mouth of the river to cut them off. Pontiac immediately went forward, and by means of that remarkable influence he ever exercised over his ferocious kinsmen, persuaded the Indians to abandon their intention.

When Rogers entered the Detroit river, he sent one of his men forward to Captain Beletree, with a copy of the capitulation, requiring that the place should be given up in accordance with its provisions. The French commander stormed and raved, and, at first, refused submission. He did all he could to incite the Indians to attack the English; but his efforts proved useless, and he was compelled to surrender with the best grace possible. On the 29th of November, 1760, about one century ago, Major Rogers took formal possession of Detroit. The lily of France was lowered, and the cross of St. George run up in its place. The garrison were sent as prisoners down the lake, and the surrounding Canadian settlers, swearing allegiance to Great Britain, were allowed to retain their farms and houses. The thousands of Indians who beheld a great number of French surrender to a handful of English, viewed the proceeding with the most wondering amazement. They believed the latter to be the bravest nation of the world, and hailed their advent with the most frenzied yells of admiration.

CHAPTER I

IMPRUDENT CONDUCT OF THE ENGLISH—INSTIGATIONS OF THE FRENCH—ALARM OF CAPTAIN CAMPBELL—THE SULPHUROUS STORM—PONTIAC AND HIS EMBASSADORS—SIR WILLIAM JOHNSON—FORT MIAMI—TREATY AT PARIS

Now that Canada was in possession of the English, and she had thrown feeble garrisons into all of the extreme western posts, it might well be supposed that every thing would be done to retain the good-will of the Indians. This was an easy task, as the savages had welcomed their coming with the most boisterous manifestations of joy; but, with an unaccountable blindness, the new masters of the country failed to see their own interests. Hitherto the Indians had been treated with indifference, now they were scorned and insulted. Their annual presents were either withheld or were meted out with a niggardly hand. In many cases Government agents first appropriated these presents to themselves, and then sold them at infamous prices to their allies and dependents. The French, entering a new country, always presented their red friends with guns, ammunition and blankets. Thus the savages became, in a measure, dependent upon them. The sudden stoppage of these presents by the English occasioned much suffering and discontent; while, to aggravate growing dislike, the English Government licensed, as fur traders, a set of unscrupulous men, who took every advantage of the Indians, who received their remonstrances with blows and curses, and left nothing undone which could inflame their hatred. Ere long the English found inveterate enemies in all the tribes by which they were surrounded.

The French, smarting under their humiliation, witnessed this growing discontent with the greatest pleasure. Knowing that Canada was irrecoverably gone, they found consolation in the thought of Indian revenge upon their rivals and enemies. Accordingly they fed these murmurings, never neglected to slander the English, assuring the savages that the determination of the conquerors was to uproot the Indian race, and that their only hope lay in a firm opposition to their schemes

The French explained their seeming weakness in yielding up the country, by saying that the King of France had been asleep, but he was now awakened, and was sending his armies up the St. Lawrence and Mississippi to drive their enemies from the country.

About this time, a prophet appeared among the Delawares, who incited the Indians to rebellion. He besought them to lay aside all the weapons received from the whites, to return to their original state, when power would be given them to drive every invader from the country. These mutterings of discontent it must not be imagined were confined merely to the vicinity of Detroit. The encroachments of the settlers in other parts of the country were continued. The Delawares and Shawnees especially were in a state of absolute frenzy, only waiting for the proper moment to burst upon the defenseless settlers. "From the head of the Potomac to Lake Superior, and from the Alleganies to the Mississippi, in every wigwam and hamlet of the forest, a deep rooted hatred of the English increased with rapid growth." A guiding spirit only was wanted—that guiding spirit was destined to be PONTIAC CHIEF OF THE OTTAWAS.

In the summer of 1761, Captain Campbell, then commander of Detroit, was told that a deputation of Senecas had visited the neighboring Wyandots, inciting them to destroy the garrison. Campbell's suspicions had been aroused, for some time, and he immediately investigated the report, to find that there was a general plot by which Forts Pitt, Niagara and others were to share the same fate as Detroit. He quickly dispatched runners to the different posts, and took such precautions that this, the first conspiracy, was crushed out before it had fully ripened.* The succeeding summer, a precisely

---

* "SIR:— { DETROIT, June 17th, 1761,
{ 2 o'clock in the morning.

"I had the favor of yours, with General Amherst's Dispatches.

"I have sent you an Express with a very Important piece of Intelligence, I have had the good Fortune to Discover. I have been Lately alarmed with Reports of the bad Designs of the Indian Nations against this place and the English in General, I can now Inform You for certain it comes from the Six Nations, and that they have Sent Belts of Wampum & Deputys to all their Nations, from Nova Scotia to the Illinois, to take up the Hatchet against the English, & have Employed the Messengers to send Belts of Wampum to the Northern Nations.

"Their project is as follows, the Six Nations—at least the Senecas are to Assemble at the head of French Creek, within five and twenty Leagues

similar plot was discovered, and, in the same manner, frustrated

But these were only the faint mutterings of the thunder in the far-off horizon. Unseen but subtle elements were rapidly uniting in every part of the sky, and the whole heavens were soon to burst forth in one blaze of destroying fire. A storm, such as the North American continent had never before witnessed was marshaling its forces, and its awful gloom was already darkening the land

It is stated that a few days before Philip of Mount Hope rushed forth at the head of his Narragansett warriors, the New England Puritans saw the figure of an Indian bow in the sky, and the shadow of a human scalp upon the moon's disk. In the autumn of 1762, clouds of midnight blackness settled over the settlement and fort of Detroit. Rain of a sulphurous odor, and of such dark color fell, that it is reported to have been gathered and used for writing purposes!* A phenomenon that philosophers have attempted to explain upon some principle of meteorologic science, was a dire portent to the simple minded Canadian. All through the following winter, around their hearth-stones, they conversed about it in subdued voices, and all agreed that a gloomy future awaited them.

The fort and settlement of Detroit, at this time, numbered about twenty five hundred souls. They stood on the western side of Detroit river. The fort, or fortified part of the town, was directly in the center of the settlement, and contained about one hundred houses placed compactly together, and surrounded by a palisade. Above and below, for six or eight miles, the stream was lined with the cabins of the Canadians. These latter, it must be borne in mind, are not included in that part of the town which was besieged, as their inhabitants, being French, remained on good terms with the Indians

of Presqu'Isle, part of the Six Nations, the Delawars and Shanese, are to Assemble on the Ohio, and all at the same time about the latter End of the Month, to surprise Niagara and Fort Pitt, and Cut off the Communication Everywhere. I hope this will Come Time enough to put You on Your Guard and to send to Oswego and all the Posts on that communication, they Expect to be Joined by the Nations that are Come from the North of Toronto ——"

Captain Campbell, Commander at Detroit to Captain Walters Commander at Niagara

* Gentleman's Magazine, XXXIV, 103. Carver's Travels, 153

The fort and palisaded center of the settlement were the portions occupied by the English, and against them the fire of the savages was directed.

It has never been known which tribe opened hostilities, but it is generally believed that Kiashuta, chief of the Senecas and one of the leading men of the Six Nations, took the initiatory step, by attacking Fort Pitt. Pontiac, however, had opened the way, and he alone, on the side of the Indians, is responsible for the war. Without the guidance of his masterly mind, it would have ended with the first demonstration.

Pontiac, by the force of his own genius, had risen to be the supreme head of the Ottawas, Ojibwas and Pottawatomies who occupied both sides of the river around Detroit. No chief dared to oppose him. Even tribes in Illinois, to the furthest limits of the Algonquin race, reverenced his name and obeyed his will. In gifts, genius, influence and vaulting ambition, he only finds a parallel in the renowned Shawnee chief, Tecumseh. At the moment of hostilities at Detroit he was about fifty years of age, of a strong, well-developed frame, a finely poised head, and an eye as keen as the eagle's. All were moved by a mind of exhaustless resource, and a will as firm as the unyielding oak of his native forests.

His dignity, determination, courage, address, surpassing eloquence and extraordinary aims had given him boundless power over the wild denizens of the forest. He seemed to impersonate the spirit of Vengeance, and inspired in his followers the reverence which only a master-soul can compel. So lasting was that influence, that, to this day, the name Pontiac is reverently pronounced by Algonquin lips.

Every thing being in readiness for the long meditated scheme of deliverance, the chieftain no longer hesitated. In the winter of 1762, while the inky storm was the subject of every tongue, he sent his embassadors to the tribes on the Ohio, to the upper lakes, and as far south as the mouth of the Mississippi. They bore with them an enormous war-belt of wampum, so important was the occasion, and a blood-red tomahawk (the sign of war) which was flung on the ground, while, with excited gestures the leading embassador addressed the assembled chiefs and warriors, in the words which Pontiac had instructed him. Everywhere the belt was welcomed, hatchet caught up, and the chiefs pledged themselves for war. Not a tribe demurred. All were anxious to strike the blow. It was therefore finally determined that the uprising should occur in the following May.

The Indians thus pledged, comprised, with the exception of one or two small tribes, the entire Algonquin family, including also the Wyandots and Senecas. The remaining members of the Six Nations were kept from joining in the Conspiracy by the influence of the excellent Sir William Johnson.*

Not the least wonderful fact of this gigantic uprising, was the skill and secrecy with which it was matured. While the thousands of savages that surrounded the whites were concocting their schemes of destruction, the latter, save in a few exceptional cases, had no intimation of the threatened danger. The lazy Indians still lounged around the fort, begging for "tobac," whisky or ammunition, their faces, so far as discernible beneath their coat of grease and dirt, wearing the same stolid expression of brutish indifference. Now and then, perhaps, when some imprudent soldier kicked the savage in his way, the snakish eyes of the "son of the forest" would glitter with a malignant blackness, and menacing his insulter's back, he would mutter something about "kill,—burn,—scalps." Perchance some intoxicated half breed let out a dark hint about adorning his hunting frock with English hair, or some brooding Frenchman checked the boasting Englishman with the meaning remark that Detroit might change masters ere long. This was all, however, that the English could afterward recall of warning of the meditated massacre of their race.

In March, 1763, a friendly Indian told Ensign Holmes, at Fort Miami, that a war belt had just been received by the

* This man was an Irishman who emigrated to America in 1734, and when but nineteen years of age, took charge of an extensive tract of land in New York Province, belonging to a relative. He accumulated wealth rapidly, and built two large mansions, one of which (Johnson Hall) is still standing in Johnstown. He settled in Mohawk valley and became a great favorite with the surrounding Indians. In the war of 1755, he was made a Major-General and commanded the colonial troops at the battle of Lake George. For his brilliant victory he was made a baronet, and given five thousand pounds by his king. He was, shortly after, appointed Superintendent of Indian Affairs, and in 1759 when General Prideaux was killed before Niagara he took his place, and routed the French for the second time. After the treaty of 1765 he remained at Johnson Hall, surrounded by numerous tenantry, who greatly loved him. He died 1774.

savages of a neighboring village and they had been urged to destroy the garrison. He added, also, that the Indians were making preparations to do it. Holmes instantly called them together and charged them with the treachery. They confessed to having been instigated to commit the deed, but expressed great sorrow and pledged eternal good-will in future. Holmes sent the tidings to Major Gladwyn, who, in turn, carefully considered the circumstances, and, while Pontiac, the life and being of the Conspiracy, was scarcely a mile above him, he sent a letter to Sir Jeffrey Amherst, stating the particulars, adding that, in all probability, the affair would soon blow over, and that it was hardly worth while to give any further concern regarding it.

The winter passed without any thing further occurring to spread direct alarm in the fort. Numerous reports,—gloomy, fearful and vague, reached the garrison, but the Indians around Detroit and the other forts manifested no noticeable change in their conduct. As spring approached, they gathered in small parties around the different posts, usually encamping in the woods at night. More definite rumors finally came from the settlements. Perhaps some wounded trader tottered into a fort with the tidings that his party had been attacked and all slain but himself, or some returning hunter reported the woods full of warlike bands of Indians. Then came the dreadful tidings that every post had fallen and all the inhabitants massacred! Although this proved false, the hardly less startling fact was made known that the bloody work had already been commenced, further south.

In February, 1763, the treaty at Paris was signed. By this, France, as before stated, yielded all claims to the territory east of the Mississippi, while England commanded her subjects to leave the Ohio valley and adjacent regions as an Indian domain, issuing a proclamation to that effect, on the 7th of October. Had this been done a year sooner, the great Conspiracy in all probability would have never been entered into. But the remedy came too late. While negotiations were pending in the courts of Europe, thousands of infuriated Indians in the wilds of North America were chanting their war-song, dancing their war-dance, and preparing their weapons for a conflict which should cause the hearts of strong men to stand still at its recital.

CHAPTER II.

PONTIAC HOLDS A COUNCIL—VISITS THE GARRISON WITH HIS SPIES—THE PLAN OF THE CONSPIRACY AGREED UPON—SUSPICIOUS PROCEEDINGS NOTED—GLADWYN WARNED BY M GOUIN—IS NOT ALARMED—THE PLOT REVEALED BY AN OJIBWA GIRL—PREPARATIONS FOR THE ATTACK

On the 27th of April, Pontiac called a council of the different tribes to meet on the river Ecorces, a short distance from Detroit At the appointed time, the wild and almost naked Ojibwas, the Ottawas with their picturesque blankets drawn closely around them, and the Wyandots in their painted shirts, and feathered hair, seated themselves upon the ground in different circles and gravely awaited the commencement of ceremonies.

First, the pipes with ornamented stems were lighted, and passed from mouth to mouth, then Pontiac walked deliberately forward into the midst of the council Though ordinarily dressed in the simple attire of his followers, he was now plumed and painted in a manner becoming his high station. Looking around upon the faces of his different auditors, his black eye shone with unwonted fierceness. He commenced speaking in an impassioned voice, pouring forth his indignation upon the English for their arrogance and insults He compared their severe conduct with the kind treatment of the French, and asserted that unless they were driven from the country the Indians would soon be utterly exterminated Then, holding up the broad belt of wampum, he stated that it had been received from the King of France, whose sleep was now ended, and who, at that moment, was on his way with his big war-canoes to drive the intruders from the country. Having wrought his listeners up to the highest pitch of excitement, he changed his voice, and in a low, deep and thrilling tone related the following story —

"A Delaware Indian conceived an eager desire to learn wisdom from the Master of Life, but, being ignorant where to find him, he had recourse to fasting, dreaming, and magical incantations. By these means it was revealed to him, that, by moving forward in a straight, undeviating course, he would reach the abode of the Great Spirit. He told his purpose to no one, and having provided the equipments of a hunter,—gun, powder-horn, ammunition, and a kettle for preparing his food,—he set forth on his errand. For some days he journeyed on in high hope and confidence. On the evening of the eighth day he stopped by the side of a brook at the edge of a small prairie, where he began to make ready his evening meal, when, looking up, he saw three large openings in the woods on the opposite side of the meadow, and three well-beaten paths which entered them. He was much surprised; but his wonder increased when, after it had grown dark, the three paths were more clearly visible than ever. Remembering the important object of his visit, he could neither sleep nor rest; and, leaving his fire, he crossed the meadow, and entered the largest of the three openings. He had advanced but a short distance into the forest, when a bright flame sprung out of the ground before him, and arrested his steps. In great amazement, he turned back, and entered the second path, where the same wonderful phenomenon again encountered him; and now, in terror and bewilderment, yet still resolved to persevere, he pursued the last of the three paths. On this he journeyed a whole day without interruption when, at length, emerging from the forest, he saw before him a vast mountain of dazzling whiteness. So precipitous was the ascent, that the Indian thought it hopeless to go further, and looked around him in despair: at that moment, he saw, seated at some distance above, the figure of a beautiful woman arrayed in white, who arose as he looked upon her, and thus accosted him. 'How can you hope, encumbered as you are, to succeed in your design? Go down to the foot of the mountain, throw away your gun, your ammunition, your provisions, and your clothing, wash yourself in the stream which flows there, and you will then be prepared to stand before the Master of Life.' The Indian obeyed, and again began to ascend among the rocks, while the woman, seeing him still discouraged, laughed at his faintness of heart, and told him that, if he wished for success, he must climb by the aid of one foot and one hand only. After great toil and suffering, he at length found himself at the summit. The woman had disappeared, and he was left alone. A rich and beautiful plain lay before him, and at a little distance, he saw three great villages, far superior to the squalid dwellings of the Delawares. As he approached the largest, and stood hesitating whether he should enter, a man gorgeously attired stepped forth, and taking him by the hand, welcomed him to the celestial abode. He then conducted him into the presence of the Great Spirit, where the Indian stood confounded at the unspeakable splendor which surrounded him. The Great Spirit bade him be seated, and thus addressed him:—

"'I am the Maker of heaven and earth, the trees, lakes, rivers, and all things else; I am the maker of mankind; and because I love you, you must do my will. The land on which you lived was made for you, and not for others. Why do you suffer the white men to dwell among you? My children, you have forgotten the customs and traditions of your forefathers. Why do you not clothe yourself in skins, as they did, and use the bows and arrows, and the stone-pointed lances, which they used? You have bought guns, knives, kettles, and blankets from the white men, until you can no longer do without them, and what is worse, you have drunk the poison fire-water, which turns you into fools. Fling all these things away, live as your wise forefathers lived before you. And as for these English,—these dogs dressed in red, who have come to rob you of your hunting grounds, and drive away the game,—you must lift the hatchet against them. Wipe them from the face of the earth, and then you will win my favor back again, and once more be happy and prosperous. The children of your great father, the King of France, are not like the English. Never forget that they are your brethren. They are very dear to me, for they love the red men, and understand the true mode of worshiping me.'

"The Great Spirit next instructed his hearer in various precepts of morality and religion, such as the prohibition to marry more than one wife, and a warning against the practice of magic, which is worshiping the devil. A prayer, embodying the substance of all that he had heard, was then presented to the Delaware. It was cut in hieroglyphics upon a wooden stick, after the custom of his people, and he was directed to send copies of it to all the Indian villages.

"The adventurer now departed, and returning to the earth, reported all the wonders he had seen in the celestial regions.*"

The Indian is naturally superstitious, and this dream or offspring of Pontiac's heated imagination, in all probability was as implicitly believed to be a direct revelation from the Great Spirit by himself as by his followers. It will be noticed that one of the peculiar ideas it is intended to enforce is that of inducing the Indians to return to their primitive condition—to reject every thing received from the English and use only the weapons they had possessed before they ever saw a white man. This is in perfect keeping with the Indian character. It was afterward one of the favorite ideas with Tecumseh and many other distinguished chiefs.

At the conclusion, as Pontiac expected, he found the Indians eager to attack the British garrison. He told them that on the second of May, under pretense of performing the calumet dance before the fort, they would gain admittance for a large

* Parkman

party, note carefully the strength and preparations of the fort, when another council would be held and the mode of assault settled upon

The council now broke up. In the morning, in accordance with a long observed custom, the Indians moved up the river and took up their encampment within a short distance of Detroit. A few days after (the first of May) Pontiac, at the head of forty Ottawas, made his appearance before the gate and asked permission to enter and perform the calumet dance before the officers. There was some debate and hesitation before admitting him; but, as no just cause could be given for refusing, the gate was thrown open and the warriors stalked into the village. Walking to the front of Major Gladwyn's house, Pontiac, with thirty of the Ottawas, instantly commenced the noisy dance, while the ten others wandered into the fort, as if by accident. Their listless manner failed to attract the attention of a single soldier, whose minds seemed wholly absorbed in witnessing the grotesque performance of the others at the corner of the street. But not an object escaped these spies. Behind the black, horse like hair that dangled in their faces, their glowing eyes were constantly flitting hither and thither, resting upon even the smallest preparation, and taking in with an unerring accuracy the strength of the little garrison. Their object being accomplished they withdrew and gradually mixed in with their yelling confederates in the street. Soon after the whole body passed out of the fort, without awakening in the minds of either officers or men, a single suspicion of the true cause of their visit.

So soon as all the Indians could be notified, a council of the principal chiefs was called in the Pottawatomie village. In the dimly lighted council-house were seated over a hundred sachems. The sacred pipe passed from mouth to mouth until all had smoked. Sentinels were stationed on the outside to prevent interruption. When the proper moment arrived Pontiac arose and unfolded his treacherous scheme. It proposed that a council should be demanded of Major Gladwyn on matters of the utmost importance. By this means, he believed he and the principal chiefs would gain admittance, with their arms concealed beneath their blankets. Pontiac would address the commandant, and, at the close of his speech, present him with a belt of wampum. This was to be the signal for all the chiefs to rush upon the officers present and strike them down. A large body of Indians would be loitering upon the outside, who, upon hearing the discharge of guns, would rush in and assail the soldiers, and thus, it was believed, Detroit would be a certain and easy prey.

The chiefs received the proposal with hoarse grunts of approval, and, gathering their blankets around them departed to prepare for the execution of the deep-laid plan.

An unaccountable sense of security pervaded the garrison. The dark, ominous storm of the winter before was forgotten, or failed of its first effect upon their minds. The Indians still lounged around the fort in large numbers, as persistently begging for whisky, tobacco and ammunition; the soldiers treated them in the same reckless, insulting manner. On the fifth of May a Canadian woman (Mrs. Aubun) visited the Ottawa village for the purpose of procuring some maple sugar. She was struck at noticing that most of the Indians were engaged in filing off their gun barrels, so as to shorten them nearly one-half.

Returning home she mentioned the fact to several of her neighbors, when one of them, a blacksmith, remarked that there had been large numbers at his shop for a day or two, asking for files and saws for some purpose which they refused to reveal.* This circumstance aroused the suspicions of several of the Canadians that something was going wrong, and they proceeded to notify Major Gladwyn. Some of the lower classes of the Canadians must have been aware of the plot, and could have revealed it, if they chose; but it is generally believed that the better class knew nothing of the conspiracy until it was upon them, or they would have disclosed it. M Gouin, one of the wealthiest settlers, hearing the blacksmith's story, went to Major Gladwyn and told him to be upon his guard, as there was every reason to believe that a deep plot

---

* In 1824 General Cass, wishing to write an account of the siege of Detroit, caused numerous inquiries to be made among the aged Canadians, many of whom distinctly remembered the incidents. Lieutenant Aubun, the son of the woman mentioned, was fifteen years old at the time and related with great minuteness many of the events. He recollected the visit of his mother, and remembered often seeing Pontiac at his head quarters at the house of Meloche.

was brewing among the Ottawas.* Gladwyn thanked his informer, but laughed at his fears and regarded the suspicions as without the slightest foundation.

His disbelief, however, was soon removed by a direct revelation of the whole plot. In the Pottawatomie village lived an Ojibwa girl who was the mistress of Major Gladwyn, and who loved him with the whole warmth of her generous soul. On the afternoon of the day, following the warning of M. Gouin, she came into the fort with a pair of elk skin moccasins as a present to the commander. He noticed the pensive and saddened look she wore, but said nothing about it, and she withdrew. Still she lingered on the street, as if loth to depart until she had relieved her mind of some burden that was oppressing it. The sentinel, noticing her singular conduct, mentioned it to Gladwyn, who, recalling the girl, pressed her to reveal the cause of her trouble. She refused for a time to make any reply; but, after much urging and many promises not to betray her, she disclosed the whole murderous scheme. She said that on the morrow Pontiac, accompanied by sixty chiefs, would come to the fort. Each of these would have a short musket concealed under his blanket. Pontiac would make a speech as before mentioned, and, at its close, offer a peace belt of wampum, holding it in a reversed position. This would be the signal for the chiefs to shoot down the officers, and for the Indians upon the outside to commence the bloody work. The French were to be spared, but every Englishman was to be massacred.

This was certainly enough to alarm any one, and Major Gladwyn concluded it was time for his preparations to be made. He thanked the faithful, loving girl, promising that she should be rewarded, but advised her to return to the village to prevent any suspicions being excited in regard to her. Calling in his subordinates he related what had transpired. He knew the defenses were too weak to repel a general assault, and was fearful the Indians might attack them during the

* M. Gouin, another of General Cass's informants, was the son of this Canadian settler. Although but eleven years old at the time, he remembered the siege with great distinctness. He often saw Pontiac, and spoke of him as possessing the most extraordinary power over his followers. The father of M. Gouin was one of the most influential traders in the settlements, and more than once acted the part of mediator between the English and Indians.

night. Every possible preparation was made. Half the garrison were put under arms, and the other half spent the night upon the ramparts. The sentinels knew not why their strength was doubled, nor had the men any idea of the true danger that threatened them. At intervals through the night, Major Gladwyn mounted the ramparts, and spent many long, anxious minutes in endeavoring to pierce the surrounding gloom. Nothing disturbed the quiet appearance of the forest, but, now and then, the soft night-wind brought faintly to his ears the sounds of yells and drums in the distance—sure evidence of the truth of what the Ojibwa maiden had told him.

NOTE.—A curious document, supposed to be a diary kept by a French priest, during this memorable siege, and known as the "Pontiac Manuscript," was preserved by a Canadian family at Detroit, and is now in possession of the Historical Society in Michigan. Contrary to all other accounts, it states that Pontiac's Conspiracy was disclosed to Major Gladwin by a *man* of the Ottawa tribe, but, in regard to the girl mentioned, it says that she was seized upon suspicion, by Pontiac's orders—failing, however, to add whether she was punished or not. An old Indian, who, for many years, was United States interpreter at Detroit, stated that Pontiac himself gave her a severe beating, but that she lived many years afterward and, getting into bad habits, in her old age, she one day fell into a kettle of boiling sap, and was so badly scalded that she soon died.

CHAPTER III.

PONTIAC BAFFLED—HOSTILITIES—THE WAR DANCE—DEATH OF CAPTAIN ROBERTSON AND SIR ROBERT DAVERS—PONTIAC JOINED BY THE OJIBWAS—DEFENSES OF DETROIT—THE ATTACK—BETRAYAL OF MAJOR CAMPBELL AND LIEUTENANT M'DOUGAL—PONTIAC COMPELS THE WYANDOTS TO JOIN HIM—ATTACK RENEWED.

THE sun had hardly risen when the common behind the fort was filled with warriors, squaws and children. They were excited and restless, and appeared to be making preparations for a general game of ball. Several applied for admission, and Gladwyn did not refuse, it being his wish to let the Indians know their plot was detected and their intentions held in contempt. Shortly after, Pontiac was seen approaching, at the head of sixty warriors, all marching in

Indian file. Just previous to this, a Canadian named Beaufait had started homeward. He met these savages at the bridge leading over Bloody Creek, and stepped aside to allow them to pass. As the last one in the file came up to him, the white recognized him as an old friend. The savage saluted him,—then carefully lifting the fold of his blanket, revealed the concealed gun, intimating, at the same time, by a meaning gesture toward the fort, what their intentions were in regard to it.*

Near the middle of the forenoon these warriors appeared before the gate, and Pontiac demanded admission. The gate was opened and they filed in. Pontiac instinctively looked about him as he entered, and the start he made when he saw the evidences of preparation upon every hand, was noticed by all. His habitual stoicism could not conceal the chagrin he felt when made aware that his treachery was discovered. On either side were drawn up ranks of armed soldiers, the fierce-looking fur-traders armed to the teeth, while the meaning tap of the drum was heard in the streets. Smothering his indignation by a great effort, he strode through the town to the door of the council-house, standing on the margin of the river, where he was allowed to enter, followed by his chiefs. Within the building Pontiac found Major Gladwyn and his officers seated ready to receive him. It did not escape the eyes of the chief that every man's belt held a pair of pistols, and every sword was in its place.

"Why do I see so many of my father's men standing with their guns in the street?" demanded Pontiac.

"They are ordered under arms for the purpose of discipline," replied Major Gladwyn through his interpreter.

Pontiac said nothing further, but it was plainly evident that he was dissatisfied with this explanation, and was in a dilemma at the attitude of things. Soon, however, the chiefs seated themselves upon the mats, and, after the usual pause, Pontiac arose to speak, holding in his hand the belt of wampum.

What an exciting moment! On the floor, in several circles, sat the sixty warriors, their blankets drawn closely around their throats, each shielding a weapon charged with death.

* This incident is given in Cass's Discourse before the Michigan Historical Society. It was related to the General by the son of Beaufait.

Some wore plumes made from the hawk, raven or eagle's wings, others had nothing but the long scalp lock dangling from their crown. Their cheeks were daubed with vermilion, ocher and soot, while their orbs gleamed and scintillated like those of the rattlesnake. In the center, and a little in advance, stood Pontiac—their leader—holding the all-important wampum belt in one hand, while the other was raised to give force to his words. A few feet distant were seated Major Gladwyn and his officers, their eyes immovably fixed upon the Ottawa chief, while his speech was scarcely heard. A single movement of that upraised arm, they knew would be the signal for an instant and deadly conflict between those who were now so calmly confronting each other. Once, it is said, Pontiac raised the belt, but a sudden rattle of arms, and the din of the rolling drum, made him lower it again. How the hearts of officers and men must have throbbed! How the chests of those red tigers must have heaved, as the torch was thus dallied within a few inches of the powder-mine!

Pontiac, completely perplexed and outwitted, sat down with the wampum-belt in his hand, and Major Gladwyn arose to reply. His words were brief, but to the point. He said that, as long as the Indians deserved the friendship of the English they should have it, but, the first treacherous act would be followed by a prompt retaliation. The council then broke up. The doors were flung open, and, as the chiefs were about to pass out, Pontiac told Gladwyn that he should visit the fort again in a few days, accompanied by his squaws and children, that they might shake hands with the English. Gladwyn made no reply, and the savages were soon again outside the fort.

The next morning, Pontiac reappeared at the fort with three of his chiefs, carrying the calumet of peace. Offering it to Gladwyn, he said:—

'My father, evil birds have sung lies in your ears. We who stand before you are friends of the English. We love you as our brothers, and have now come to smoke the pipe of peace with you.'

When all had smoked he presented it to Major Campbell, as a further pledge of friendship. In the afternoon of the same day, Pontiac called all the young men to a game of ball, which took place near the fort. At its close, the victorious party set up loud yells which so alarmed the officers that the drums were beat to quarters; but the alarm shortly passed off when the true cause was made known.

On Monday, the ninth of May, the common behind the fort was once more thronged with Indians from the four different tribes. Pontiac advanced from the midst and demanded admittance at the gate.

"You may enter yourself, if you choose," said Gladwyn, "but no one else can come in."

"I wish *all* my warriors to enjoy the friendly calumet," said the chief.

"*All* your warriors shall not do it, and no one besides you shall enter as long as we can keep them out," rejoined Gladwyn.

Pontiac saw that it was useless to undertake to conceal his designs any longer. With an expression of the deadliest hate, he turned and strode toward his warriors, who, at his approach sprung up and ran off "yelping like so many devils."

The Indians were seen running rapidly toward a house where an English woman and her two sons lived. They beat down the door and poured in like a swarm of bees. A moment after, the dismal scalp-yell announced the fate of the inmates. A number of them then started on a rapid run down the river-bank. Springing into their canoes they paddled rapidly toward the Isle au Cochon. Here lived an Englishman, formerly a Sergeant of the regulars, named Fisher. He was immediately seized, murdered and scalped, and with many yells of exultation, the savages left the island.

The next day, several Canadians crossed over to the island and buried the body. But upon visiting the spot the next day they saw the hands of the murdered man protruding from the ground, as if in an attitude of entreaty. They buried him more effectually, but upon returning a second time, to their horror, they saw the hands again. They repaired to a priest who visited the island and performed the neglected rites, after which the corpse reposed in peace.*

Pontiac, when repulsed by Gladwyn, turned to the shore

---

* This circumstance is well supported by tradition. Lieutenant Aubin asserted to General Cass that it was true in every particular. Such an occurrence, it can be seen, could take place without any supernatural agency.

None dared to approach him, so awful was his rage. Stepping into a canoe, he impelled it up stream toward the Ottawa village. As he drew near he shouted to the inhabitants. They all rushed forth, old men, women and children. He ordered them to move their camp to the western shore, that the river should no longer be between them and the English. They set to work at once so assiduously, that by night-fall every thing, even the bark-covering to their lodges, was ready for transportation. By this time the Indians had returned from their murders, and as they gathered around Pontiac, covered with his war-paint, bounded into the open space in the center of the assembly. Swinging his tomahawk over his head, and stamping the ground, he commenced a wild and loud harangue—relating his various services and exploits, and ended by vowing vengeance upon the hated English foe. The others caught his wild enthusiasm, and shortly all were circling around and around, giving vent to yells that went down over the waters like the notes of vengeance to the garrison.

The war-dance finished, the work of removal commenced. Before daybreak the Ottawa village stood on the western side of Detroit, just above the mouth of Parent's creek, and about a mile and a half above the garrison. (This creek is now known as Bloody Run. It is indicated on the accompanying map as the scene of Dalzell's fight.)

In the evening, a Canadian coming down the river landed at the fort, bringing the sad tidings that two English officers, Captain Robertson and Sir Robert Davers, had been murdered by the Indians above Lake St. Clair. He stated, also, that the Ojibwas of Saginaw Bay, a most bloodthirsty set, had united with Pontiac.

Major Gladwyn now began to entertain an adequate idea of the danger which threatened his little garrison. Hitherto he had believed it to be only a temporary outbreak which must soon be quieted, but it now was plain that the disaffection was general and that a most dreadful fate menaced all the Western forts.

Major Gladwyn took a careful survey of the defenses of the place. The center of the town, it will be recollected, was inclosed by pickets, nearly in the form of a square. At the corners and over the gates were block-houses, while an open space intervened between the houses and pickets. The fortifications did not reach to the river, but a gate opened in the direction of the stream, where, at this time, most fortunately indeed, two armed vessels lay at anchor. The ordnance of the fort consisted of two six pounders, one three-pounder and three mortars, all of which were of an indifferent quality. The garrison numbered one hundred and thirty, including the officers. Besides these, were some thirty or forty traders in the place; but the inadequateness of this entire force will be seen, when it is known that the stockade which surrounded the town was over a thousand feet in length.

Not a man lay down to sleep during the night, and Gladwyn himself walked the ramparts until morning. Just as the light of day was breaking over the scene, the dreadful warwhoop was sounded, and the whole host of Ottawas, Ojibwas Wyandots and Pottawatomies, came bounding from the wood like so many wolves. Their bullets rattled like hail against the palisades, and the soldiers expected a rush against their defenses. But, peering through the loop-holes, it was discovered that their assailants were not so excited as to forget to use caution in exposing their persons. Each had his mouth full of bullets and all were firing—every fence, barn, bush tree and hollow was a flame. The incessant crashing of their rifles was hardly more deafening than their demoniac yells. Behind an adjoining hill, a multitude of tufted heads were constantly appearing and vanishing, while the reports of their guns were incessant. Still nearer was a barn which seemed packed with the inhuman scoundrels, judging from the fire that came from it. To dislodge these, several handfuls of red hot spikes were thrown down a cannon and fired at the barn. The combustible material caught instantly, and in a moment the building was wrapped in flames. The Indians, in the greatest terror went leaping, yelling and dodging for other shelter, making such grotesque figures that the whole garrison broke out into hearty laughter.

For six hours the firing was kept up, when the Indians withdrew, having suffered but a trifling loss, while the garrison had only five wounded. Gladwyn at this time had but three weeks' provision in the fort. Desirous of obtaining more, he concluded to open negotiations with Pontiac, under cover of which he hoped to obtain the needed supplies. Accordingly La Butte, the interpreter, (who being a Frenchman may be said to have held a neutral position between the English and Indians) was sent to Pontiac to demand reasons for the attack Chapeton and Godfroy, two old Canadians, volunteered to accompany him in order to assist in the negotiation.

Pontiac received them kindly, and listened respectfully to the message of La Butte. At its conclusion, Chapeton and Godfroy made an earnest remonstrance with the chief, doing their utmost to persuade him from continuing the hostilities. Pontiac, with the courtesy that always distinguished him, uttered assent to all that was said, and La Butte believing perfect success would crown their efforts, withdrew for a time, that his presence might be no restraint to the two Canadians. He was deeply mortified, however, upon returning, to find that their arguments had produced no effect. Pontiac could not be prevailed upon to make any definite reply. He stated that he wished to hold a council with the English fathers themselves, expressing a desire that Major Campbell, second in command, should visit the camp. This old and faithful officer was greatly venerated by the Indians, and the proposal seemed perfectly natural. The embassadors, therefore, returned and reported to the commandant. Gladwyn believed it was only another of Pontiac's treacherous schemes, but Major Campbell could not suspect those with whom he had so long been friendly. He urged permission very strongly, and Gladwyn at length yielded his reluctant consent.

Lieutenant McDougal, was also granted permission to attend Campbell, and the two, accompanied by La Butte and several other Canadians, left the fort. Before this, however, M. Gouin (heretofore referred to) had moved through the Indian camp, and heard enough to satisfy him that the officers were about to enter a trap laid for them. He accordingly dispatched two men to warn them from coming, but it was too late. They had already left the gate, and the messengers could not induce them to return.

Going up the river bank, they crossed the bridge over Bloody Run, and, a little further on, came in sight of the Ottawa encampment. The instant the red uniforms of the Englishmen were seen, the Indians set up a loud outcry, and, armed with sticks and stones, rushed toward them. Pontiac quelled the tumult, and shaking the officers by the hand, led the way through the camp to a large lodge where he seated them upon mats and waited to hear what they had to communicate. Major Campbell arose, made a short speech and then sat down. Pontiac deigned no reply, and for full an hour Campbell and his friends sat in the most embarrassing silence. Unable to bear the suspense longer, he arose and signified his intention to return. Pontiac instantly signed for him to reseat himself. Campbell did so, and saw at once that they had been betrayed.

Still the gray-haired officer would not believe that any thing more than their mere retention was intended. Such, indeed, seemed the case with Pontiac. Many of his followers were eager to slay the Englishmen; but the chief would not consent. He took them as prisoners to the house of M. Meloche near Bloody Run,* where as much liberty as prudent was allowed them. A good reason for Campbell believing that Pontiac would do no more than this, was that two Ojibwas at that moment were in the power of Major Gladwyn.

La Butte, the interpreter, did not return to the fort until late in the evening. His gloomy intelligence was immediately read in his face. Two or three of the officers were unjust enough to express their suspicion that he was a party to the treachery. The interpreter, deeply mortified, left the fort, and sullen and thoughtful wandered around the streets, refusing communication with any one.

The next day Pontiac crossed the river to the Wyandot village, where a portion of the tribe had been so influenced by a Jesuit priest, that, thus far, they refused to take part in the hostility. Pontiac told them they should all be tomahawked if they remained neutral any longer. They soon joined him, and, it is said, proved the best warriors under his command.

Having now a truly formidable force at his disposal, the chief made his disposition of them. A number of Pottawatomies were concealed along the river bank, where they remained ready to cut off the approach of any supplies or reinforcements and to prevent any one leaving the fort.

* Previous to Dalzell's fight this stream was known as Parent's creek.

Another force was ordered to keep concealed near the place, when no attack was going on, and pick off every trader, or Englishman who showed himself for an instant.

These preparations were completed on the twelfth of May. On that morning, the Indians opened a hot fire upon the fort, kept it up almost without intermission until dusk, when their firing ceased. Major Gladwyn now called a council of his officers to decide what course to pursue. An interchange of views proved that nearly all were in favor of embarking for Niagara, in the vessels that lay in the river. This conclusion seemed reasonable, as their provisions, by the most rigid economy, would barely hold out but three weeks, and there was no room for believing that succor would be sent them. What troubled the officers most was the fear that the Indians would make a united onset upon the pickets. In such a case, nothing could prevent the massacre of the whole garrison. An old Canadian, who had spent many years among the savages, assured the council that there were not the least grounds for such an apprehension. Pontiac would never make or allow such an assault to be made by his warriors, as their principles of warfare were opposed to it.

The old Pennsylvania *Gazette* stated that Gladwyn was the only one who opposed the plan of embarking for Niagara, and that when his wishes were known, and their fears relieved by the Canadian, the officers agreed to a man to defend the fort to the last extremity. Whatever may have induced the change of mind, it did take place, and Gladwyn resolved to hold the place to the last.

Numbers of the soldiers sallied out from time to time and cut down the orchards and bushes, so that no shelter in the immediate proximity of the fort was afforded their assailants. In spite of their precautions, the snake like warriors would crawl through the grass to the palisade, and there shoot arrows tipped with blazing tow upon the roofs of the houses; but, each building was provided with a tank of water as especial guard against this danger, and the twists of fire were instantly extinguished. The church was most exposed, and Pontiac would have fired it, had not the French priest threatened such sacrilege with the vengeance of God.

Determined that the garrison should fall into his hands at

all hazards, he eagerly asked the French to teach him their method of approaching a fortified place, but such as possessed this knowledge prudently affected ignorance.

The immediate fear of the commandant was now in regard to provisions. Every thing that could answer for food was collected and placed in the public store-house. The men were served in close rations. Not a particle was allowed to go to waste, but, in spite of these precautions, hunger would have compelled the evacuation of the fort, had it not been for the timely assistance of a few friendly Canadians. One of these named Baby, who lived across the river, transported, under cover of night, numbers of hogs and cattle to the garrison. By this means the soldiers maintained hope and confidence, and openly defied the Indians to do their utmost.

CHAPTER IV.

WANT OF PROVISIONS—PONTIAC'S PROMISSORY NOTES—THE RELIEF EXPEDITION—ITS SAD FATE—PONTIAC'S SCHEMES AGAINST WESTERN FORTRESSES SUCCESSFUL—FALL OF FORT SANDUSKY, OF FORT ST JOSEPH, OF FORT MACKINAW, OF FORT MIAMI, OF FORT PRESQU'ISLE—MONSTROUS PERFIDY OF THE SAVAGES.

The Indians, believing the garrison could not hold out for any length of time, had neglected to provide themselves with provisions, and now began to experience the same privations that the English did. In meeting these wants, Pontiac displayed an ingenuity perfectly wonderful in an Indian. The Canadian settlers had complained of the Indians stealing their provisions and destroying their crops. The chief checked this annoyance at once, and then visited each house, inspected its contents, and told the proprietor what amount he must furnish for the sustenance of his warriors, establishing a storehouse at the same time, and appointing a director. Having no means at hand to compensate the settlers, he issued *promissory notes*, drawn upon bark and signed with the figure of an otter—the *totem* to which he belonged. It is worthy of record that every one of these notes was afterward faithfully redeemed by the remarkable debtor.

Time wore on, and the flag of Briton still floated above Detroit. The savages did not for an instant relax their watchfulness. If the head or limb of a soldier was exposed, several rifles were sure to be discharged at it, and, as has already been said, hardly a man lay down to rest at night for weeks together. The streets were deserted and quiet. Now and then some indolent Canadian, or a gaudily-dressed Indian girl, mistress of a trader or officer, would saunter along, making the gloom and desolation only the more gloomy and desolate.

Soon Gladwyn heard that a convoy was on its way to Detroit to relieve him. Impatient and anxious for its arrival, Gladwyn dispatched one of his schooners to hasten it forward. The vessel moved slowly down the river, the men fearful and almost certain of an attack from the savages before they should reach their destination. The next day, while in the very mouth of Lake Erie, the wind fell to a dead calm, and she became motionless, "as a painted ship upon a painted sea." As she lay here, the sails now and then flapping uselessly, a multitude of canoes suddenly started out from the opposite shores and made toward her. In the prow of the foremost the Indians had stationed Major Campbell, their prisoner, believing he would be a screen of safety to themselves. The gallant old officer cried out to his friends to do their duty without minding him. Fortunate indeed had it been for him had such been the case, and he had fallen by a bullet from his own countrymen; but, before the canoes could reach the schooner, her sails suddenly swelled to the wind, and she was carried safely out into the lake beyond their reach.

Long and anxiously did the garrison look for the expected convoy; the weary sentinel, pacing the ramparts, turned his eager eyes again and again to catch a glimpse of her as she rounded the bend in the river. And, as day after day, the sun disappeared without bringing any tidings, the heart sickened at the dreadful apprehensions that arose in the minds of all. But on the morning of the thirtieth of May, the sentinel shouted that the convoy had appeared! The news ran like an electric shock through the garrison. The whole place was aroused. Officers, soldiers and traders, their faces illuminated by joy, and hope gratified, crowded together, as, with swelling hearts, they watched the boats as they slowly came up the river. A perfect fleet of them was rounding Montreal Point, their ashen oars flashing in the sunlight, and the blood red cross of England gayly streaming above them. The siege, they believed, was now at an end. Men, arms and provisions were at hand, and the treacherous savages were baffled of their prey.

Nearer and nearer comes the welcome vessel, while the garrison breaks forth into three hearty cheers. Again and again they are repeated, and the soldiers become frenzied with joy. The cannons belch forth their loud welcome of friends and their defiance of enemies. The ramparts are crowded, hats are seen frantically swinging in the air, and the joyous hurrahs are echoed back for miles.

But look! The shouts cease. Hands drop suddenly and listlessly, while an expression of terror flashes across every face. Every heart seems to have stopped pulsating. The eyes of every officer, soldier and trader are riveted upon the canoes. Dark, dusky figures are seen to rise in them, and, with wild gestures and the chilling war-whoop, to return the salute. The dreadful truth is known at once. The convoy is in the hands of Pontiac and his murderous followers!

While the garrison stand paralyzed by this overwhelming misfortune, an incident occurs that, for the time, rouses them from their apathy by its thrilling interest. There were about a score of canoes, in each of which were two or more soldiers, deprived of their arms, and compelled to row by their armed captors. In the foremost of these chanced to be four soldiers and only three Indians. One of the former was acting as steersman, and, as the boat came opposite the schooner, which was still at anchor near the fort, he formed a plan of escape. One of the Indians was sitting directly in front of another soldier, and the steersman called to him in English to pitch the savage overboard. The man replied that he was not strong enough. The other then told him to change places with him, as though fatigued with rowing. The steersman stepped forward as if to take the oar, when he stooped, caught the Indian's hair in his left hand and his girdle in his right, and, by main strength, flung him overboard. The agile savage, as he felt himself lifted from his seat, twisted around with the quickness of lightning and caught the steersman by the clothes. Holding fast by one hand, and trailing alongside, he drew his knife with the other, pulled himself up out the water, and stabbed the soldier again and again. In their struggles the boat tipped to its gunwale, and the poor fellow went overboard. The contest continued in the water, the forms rising and sinking, in deadly strife, until both finally disappeared.*

The other two Indians, at the very commencement of the contest—which, indeed, was scarce a minute in length—sprung overboard, and the soldiers rowed for the fort with all their strength, shouting aloud for help. The other canoes were but a short distance behind and started instantly in pursuit, while the Indians upon shore opened a fire upon them. The light, birchen vessels of the pursuers gained with incredible rapidity. When about to give up in despair, a cannon from the vessel sent its ball plowing through the water within a few feet of the most advanced of the pursuers, while another one scattered the savages upon the bank. The soldiers were soon with the excited garrison. These men gave the dismal account of their misfortune. Lieutenant Cuyler had left Fort Niagara, on the thirteenth of May, with over ninety men and an abundance of provision and ammunition. He had coasted along the northern shore of Lake Erie without seeing a human being besides his own men, until the twenty eighth of the month, when he put ashore near the mouth of Detroit river. The boats (the convoy consisted only of comparatively small boats) were drawn upon the shore and preparations made for encampment. While a man and a boy were a short distance away cutting fire-wood, several Indians sprung upon them, and killed the boy, when the man ran into camp with the alarm. Lieutenant Cuyler instantly formed his men into line, and had scarcely done so when a destructive fire was opened upon them. Both parties stood their ground for a while, when a multitude of Wyandots poured on of the wood and attacked them with the greatest fury. Th en became panic-struck, the line was thrown into the most disgraceful confusion, and all, in a blind terror, rushed for the boats, throwing their guns from them as they ran. Five were pushed into the water

---

* M Goulu who was a boy at this ti says the Indian freed himself from the soldier, and he saw him swim

and piled full of the soldiers, while the Indians, setting two others afloat, started in pursuit. Three of the former allowed the Indians to recapture them without the least resistance. Lieutenant Cuyler, seeing his men all captured or routed, waded into the water, was taken in by one of the other two boats, which eventually made their escape to Niagara, where their disaster was reported to the commanding officer.

The fate of the sixty prisoners was even more appalling than their hopeless friends expected. When night set in, several Canadians came into the garrison, bringing vague and horrible rumors of their massacre by their inhuman captors. "Naked corpses, gashed with knives and scorched with fire, floated down on the pure waters of the Detroit, whose fish came up to nibble at the clotted blood that clung to their ghastly faces."* The "Pontiac Manuscript" before referred to, in regard to this awful affair, has the following account:

"The Indians, fearing that the other barges might escape as the first had done, changed their plan of going to the camp. They landed their prisoners, tied them, and conducted them by land to the Ottawa village, and then crossed them to Pontiac's camp, where they were all butchered. As soon as the canoes reached the shore, the barbarians landed their prisoners, one after the other, on the beach. They made them strip themselves, and then sent arrows into different parts of their bodies. These unfortunate men wished sometimes to throw themselves on the ground to avoid the arrows, but they were beaten with sticks and forced to stand up until they were dead, after which those who had not fired fell upon their bodies, cut them to pieces, cooked and ate them. On others they exercised different modes of torment by cutting their flesh with flints, and piercing them with lances. They would then cut their feet and hands off, and leave them weltering in their blood till they were dead. Others were fastened to stakes, and children employed in burning them with a slow fire. No kind of torment was left untried by these Indians. Some of the bodies were left on shore, others were thrown into the river. Even the women assisted their husbands in torturing their victims. They slitted them with their knives, and mangled them in various ways. There were, however, a few whose lives were saved, being adopted to serve as slaves."

This is sufficient to give a faint idea of the death of these men. As the sad truth became known to the besieged of

* Parkman.

Detroit, a deep gloom settled upon the spirits of all. None knew how soon they might share the fate of Lieutenant Cuyler's men. Enemies watchful, malignant, vindictive and merciless environed them on every side, and none but the arm of Omnipotence was strong enough to deliver them.

Fortune seemed to have abandoned the little garrison to its impending fate. Shortly after this, the dismal "death-halloo" was again heard among the Indians, and, upon looking out, a long line of naked savages was seen emerging from the wood, and walking across the open space near the fort. All were painted black, and each bore a scalp upon the top of a pole. It was plain that some new disaster had occurred, and the hearts of the almost hopeless soldiers sickened at the thought. Indeed, the disgusting ceremony of the savages was hardly finished, when a Canadian arrived at the fort with the intelligence that Fort Sandusky had been taken by the Wyandots, and all of the garrison slain or captured. Soon after, Major Gladwyn received a letter from the commandant, Ensign Paully, giving a whole account of the manner in which the post had fallen. Like nearly every other victory of the Indians, it was gained through the most consummate treachery. Paully himself had been given the choice of death at the stake or that of adoption by the tribe. Naturally enough he chose the latter, and at the time the letter was written was enrolled as an Ottawa warrior.

The fall of Sandusky was on the sixteenth of May. A few days later, Gladwyn learned that two powerful bands of Ojibwas had connected themselves with Pontiac. The force in the immediate vicinity of Detroit was, in consequence, nearly nine hundred.

At the mouth of St. Joseph's river, near the head of Lake Michigan, stood Fort St. Joseph, garrisoned only by fourteen soldiers under the command of Ensign Schlosser. On the twenty fifth of May this was attacked by a large band of Pottawatomie who obtained admittance in the same manner the Ottawas had done at Fort Sandusky. Eleven of the men were killed, and the remaining three, together with Schlosser, were brought before Detroit, on the fifteenth of June, by a band of Pottawatomies, who offered them in exchange for several prisoners held by Gladwyn. With considerable difficulty this exchange was effected, and from these prisoners the particulars above given were obtained by the commandant

Four days later, Father Jonois, a Roman Catholic priest, appeared before the fort, and delivered into the hands of Gladwyn a letter from Captain Etherington, commandant at Mackinaw. A copy of this letter, preserved in the State Paper Office of London, reads as follows:

"MICHILIMACKINAC, 12 June, 1763.

"SIR:—Notwithstanding what I wrote you in my last, that all the savages were arrived, and that every thing seemed in perfect tranquility, yet on the fourth instant, the Chippewas, who live in a plain near this fort, assembled to play ball, as they had done almost every day since their arrival. They played from morning until noon, then throwing their ball close to the gate, and observing Lieutenant Lesley and me a few paces out of it, they came behind us, seized and carried us into the woods.

"In the mean time, the rest rushed into the fort, where they found their squaws, whom they had previously planted there, with their hatchets hid under their blankets, which they took, and in an instant killed Lieutenant Jamet, fifteen rank and file, and a trader named Tracy. They wounded two, and took the rest of the garrison prisoners, five of whom they have since killed.

"They made prisoners all the English traders, and robbed them of every thing they had; but they offered no violence to the persons or property of any of the Frenchmen.

"When the massacre was over, Messrs Langdale and Farly, the interpreters, came down to the place where Lieutenant Lesley and me were prisoners, and on their giving themselves as security to return us when demanded, they obtained leave for us to go the fort, under a guard of savages, which gave time, by the assistance of the gentleman above mentioned, to send for the Ottawas, who came down on the first notice, and were very much displeased at what the Chippewas had done.

"Since the arrival of the Ottawas they have done every thing in their power to serve us, and with what prisoners the Chippewas had given them, and what they have bought, I have now with me Lieutenant Lesley and eleven privates, and the other four of the garrison who are yet living, remain in the hands of the Chippewas.

"The Chippewas, who are superior in number to the Ottawas, have declared in council to them that if they do not remove us out of the fort, they will cut off all communication to this post, by which means all the convoys of merchants from Montreal, La Baye, St Joseph, and the upper posts would perish. But if the news of your posts being attacked (which they say was the reason why they took up the hatchet) be false, and you can send up a strong reinforcement, with provisions, etc., accompanied by some of your savages, I believe the post might be re-established again.

"Since this affair happened, two canoes arrived from Montreal, which put it in my power to make a present to the Ottawa nation, who very well deserve any thing that can be done for them.

"I have been very much obliged to Messrs Langdale and Farli, the interpreter, is likewise to the Jesuit, for the many good offices they have done us on this occasion. The priest seems inclinable to go down to your post for a day or two, which I am very glad of, as he is a very good man, and had a great deal to say with the savages, hereabout, who will believe every thing he tells them on his return, which I hope will be soon. The Ottawas say they will take Lieutenant Lesley, me, and the eleven men which I mentioned before were in their hands, up to their village and there keep us, till they hear what is doing at your post. They have sent this canoe for that purpose."

This letter, it will be noticed was written a few days after the massacre at Mackinaw, and before the writer was aware of the desperate strait in which Detroit itself was placed. Of course Gladwyn was unable to do any thing for his unfortunate friend, and Father Jonois set out on his return with such tidings.

The next letter received by Major Gladwyn was from Lieutenant Edward Jenkins, commandant at Fort Ouatanon, which stood on the Wabash, near or upon the present site of Lafayette. This letter stated that, on the first of June, this place had fallen into the hands of the Indians, the latter first securing the persons of the commandant and several of his men, whom they had invited into their cabins under pretense of speaking with them.

Hardly had the news of this disaster reached Detroit when intelligence of the fate of Fort Miami was received. An Indian maiden saved Gladwyn's garrison, it will be recollected, but, in this case, one betrayed a fort. The commandant, Ensign Holmes, who had been suspicious for some time, was told by an Indian girl, in whom he had confidence, that a squaw lay dangerously ill a short distance away, and he was requested to go to her. While in the act of entering the cabin pointed out to him, he was shot dead by two Indians. The report of the guns was heard at the fort, and the Sergeant, with a sad want of discretion, instantly hurried out to ascertain the meaning of it. He walked directly into the trap, and was taken prisoner, with much whooping and exultation. Shortly after, the terrified soldiers were summoned to surrender by a Canadian and two white companions, who promised their lives and good treatment in case they submitted, but complete massacre if they refused. The frightened soldiers yielded at once, and were made prisoners.

The fall of Fort Miami took place on the twenty-seventh of May. On the fifteenth of the following month Fort Presqu'Isle was attacked. This fort was on the southern shore of Lake Erie, where the town of Erie now stands. The fort was of two stories, the upper projecting over the lower so that the defenders could fire down upon their assailants. The roof was steeply shelving and covered with dry shingles, so combustible that its danger had often been remarked by Ensign Christie. As a safeguard, there was an opening in the roof, protected by bullet-proof planks, through which water could be dashed upon the roof, in case it took fire.

The block house stood in the very worst situation possible. It was upon a projecting point of land, inclosed upon one side by the lake and upon the other by a brook, whose bank swelled into a ridge so steep that it afforded the best shelter for an enemy at only forty yards distant, while the bank of the lake possessed the same disadvantage upon the opposite side.

The garrison was but a handful in numbers, but they were men of tried courage, and Ensign Christie was worthy of being their leader. Rumors of the fall of other forts along the frontier had reached him, and he was not a man to be taken off his guard. At daybreak on the fifteenth of June, his little garrison saw themselves surrounded by over two hundred Indians, who had come from the vicinity of Detroit with the determination that the fort should be taken. As soon as the Indians were discovered, the soldiers hurried into the block house, and made hasty preparations for the attack. Sheltering themselves behind the natural embankments mentioned, the savages poured an unremitting fire at the loop holes and crevices, and shot arrows tipped with burning tow upon the roof. The dry shingles instantly caught the blaze, but were as instantly extinguished by the water prepared for such a contingency. Again and again was the attempt made, and again and again was it foiled, until the roof became charred, steamy and smoking. The assailants next rolled logs to the top of the embankments, where they constructed several strong breast-works from which they could fire with still more deadly effect. Balls of blazing pitch were cast upon the roof, but as soon as they struck, they were submerged in a torrent of water and rolled harmlessly to the ground.

Numbers of Indians attempted to run across and drop into the ditch which surrounded the fort, but every one was shot or badly wounded by the determined soldiers. At this point, the garrison saw dirt and stones cast up behind the breastworks, and they divined the truth at once. The Indians were undermining the fort, and the beleaguered possessed no power to prevent their sure approach.

By this time, too, the water was nearly exhausted, and the attempts to fire the building were still continued. Threatened thus by two perils which would have discouraged almost any man, Ensign Christie did not despair. It was certain death to attempt reaching the well in the parade ground, so the only hope was to sink one in the block-house itself. The boards were torn up and the work commenced. They had progressed but a few feet, when the building was found to be again on fire. The last cupful of water was cast upon it and it was extinguished. The men plied themselves with desperate energy, throwing the dirt constantly above, and fast disappearing down in the earth. Again the cry of fire is raised, and no signs of water have been reached. The diggers work like madmen, but it is useless, the precious element is still far below them, and they stop, panting and despairing. At this critical moment, a soldier springs out upon the roof, and, not heeding the bullets that rattle like hail around him, tears off the burning shingles, and with a defiant shout leaps back again unharmed. The men ply themselves again with renewed hope, and, ere the dreaded cry is raised, they have struck water.

Darkness now settles over the place, but the weary soldiers are given no rest. All night, the flashes of the guns encircle the block house by fire, while every loop hole is spouting flame and death. As morning once more dawns upon the scene, it is discovered that the breast-works have been advanced to the house of Christie, which is immediately fired. This stands so close to the block house that the men are nearly stifled by the heat. The outer walls of the block house itself smoke and peel and finally burst into flame. But the ever watchful soldiers soon extinguish it, and are still resolute to defend the place to its last extremity. All through the forenoon—the afternoon—the evening—until midnight the firing scarcely abates upon either side. The air within the block house is sulphurous, clogged and heated almost to suffocation, while the men, with begrimed faces, move about in the dark room, silent and resolute. At midnight some one calls out to the garrison in French to surrender. Christie asks for a man who speaks English, when a soldier, who having been made prisoner during the French war, and who has since spent his life among the Indians, steps forward from the breast work.

This man told Ensign Christie, that the preparations had been completed in such a manner, that the fort would be fired at the top and bottom at the same moment. He advised them to surrender, and he would guarantee their lives, while if they undertook to hold out longer they would all be burnt to death within the fort. Christie replied that he would give his final answer in the morning, and the assailants consenting, the hostilities were suspended until that time.

Ensign Christie was still resolved to defend the place as long as a shadow of hope remained. He felt that if the white man had stated truth, nothing remained but to surrender or to be burnt with the fort. In the morning, he instructed two of his men to go out, as if to treat with their enemies, but in reality to observe whether they had made such preparations against them. If they had not they were to return an evasive answer and make their way back to the fort, when the defence would be resumed; but, if it were otherwise, they were to notify him by means of a private signal. The soldiers advanced to the breast-work, when they signaled to Christie that every thing was as reported; and, as he had instructed them, demanded that two of the principal chiefs should advance half-way to the block-house where the commandant would receive them

This was done, and Christie negotiated with them for the surrender of the fort. Hopeless as was his case, he would not consent to deliver it up, unless the chiefs agreed that they might be allowed to march undisturbed to the next post. These were the capitulations and the men defiled out of the fort which they had defended with such bravery. The Indians instantly made them all prisoners and sent them to Detroit, but the indomitable Christie effected his escape, although most of his companions were put to death

The other posts soon followed the fate of Presqu'Isle, so that Detroit was the only one that held out. Pontiac daily grew more and more enraged at its obstinate resistance, and endeavored to intimidate the commandant, by saying that hundreds of other Indians would soon join him, when it would be impossible to prevent the massacre of all his men. To such threats Gladwyn uniformly returned an answer contemptuous and insulting, and Pontiac renewed his efforts, with a resolve more resolute than ever to make the haughty commandant sue for mercy

---

CHAPTER V

SECOND ATTEMPT TO RELIEVE THE GARRISON—THE SCHOONER'S VOYAGE—ITS ASSAULT BY THE SAVAGES—THEIR REPULSE—SAFE ARRIVAL AT DETROIT—FURY OF PONTIAC—INGENIOUS ATTEMPT TO DESTROY THE VESSELS—THE FIRE RAFT—PEACE ASKED BY THE WYANDOTS AND POTTAWATOMIES—SIEGE CONTINUED

The garrison now began to feel some alarm in regard to the schooner which, it will be remembered, Major Gladwyn had dispatched to Fort Niagara to hasten the convoy. This vessel had met Lieutenant Cuyler and gone on to Niagara, where she remained until that officer and a portion of his men returned to tell their tragic story. An instant order was given to fit out the schooner to return. The Lieutenant and his remaining men, together with such as could be spared from Niagara were placed on board and ordered to the relief of Detroit with all dispatch, and with a command to enter the fort at all hazards.

The vessel made her way slowly up the river, but, when in the narrowest portion, near Turkey Island, the wind failed her, and, knowing that hundreds of demon like eyes were watching his movements, the captain dropped down into the broader portion below to wait for the breeze. Here she lay several days partially becalmed; but, on the afternoon of the twenty-third, again commenced ascending the stream. The garrison noticed a great commotion among the Indians, but were unable to tell what was the cause of it, until M. Baby came into the fort, and stated that they were preparing to attack the schooner which had got under weigh. At this Major Gladwyn fired two cannon to let his friends know they still held out, and then the garrison waited with the most intense anxiety for the appearance of its friends and the long looked-for relief.

In the mean time the schooner was moving through the channel between Fighting Island and the eastern shore. At the very narrowest part, the wind again died out, and anchor was dropped. Some sixty men were on board, all eager for a regular battle with the Indians, who they knew were hovering along the shore in vast numbers. To invite an attack by the apparent weakness of the crew, the greater portion of these remained below during the day, not more than a dozen being visible upon the deck at the same time. Confident that an attack would be made before morning, the sentinels were stationed, and the men waited below ready to come up at an instant's warning.

As night slowly settled over stream and wood, nothing out of the usual order of things could be detected along the shore, though a most formidable breast-work had been erected by the Indians, a little further up, while they were only waiting for the proper moment to arrive, when they hoped to gain possession of the vessel. The latter lay quiet and motionless, a dusky figure now and then flitting across the deck, and the most death-like silence reigning over stream and shore.

Hour after hour wore away, and all remained the same. The watchful sentinels pierced the gloom on every side and listened for the slightest sound of danger. Nothing but the soft rippling of the current around the prow was heard, or the almost inaudible gurgling against the taut cable. The shores were invisible, but one of the sentinels suddenly detected dark, moving bodies upon the surface of the water. He gave the signal, and instantly the deck was filled with men, who took their stations as noiselessly as shadows. Numbers of birchen canoes, were seen cautiously approaching. Not a trigger was pulled until they were within a few yards when a hammer was struck upon the mast. Immediately the whole side of the black hull, burst forth in one blaze of living fire, with a crash like that of an earthquake. Musket and cannon-shot went hurtling among the canoes, sinking several, killing fourteen Indians, wounding still more and scattering the others like chaff. The panic-struck Indians hastened to the shore to open fire from their breast work; but, the schooner dropped down stream out of their reach, and a few days afterward passed safely through the channel, sending a broadside into the Wyandot village as she passed. Without a single man killed or wounded, they closed in beside the other schooner, under the walls of Detroit fort.

Her appearance was most timely, for she brought an abundance of men, provisions and ammunition. She brought also the welcome intelligence of the conclusion of peace between England and France. This placed the Canadians around Detroit in a different position. "Hitherto they had been, as it were, prisoners on capitulation, neutral spectators of the quarrel between their British conquerors and the Indians; but now their allegiance was transferred from the crown of France to that of Britain, and they were subjects of the English king."*

The majority of these Canadians hated the English as much as did the Indians, and they positively refused to submit to the treaty. They even declared to Pontiac that the whole story was a fabrication of Major Gladwyn's—that the King of France would never desert thus his children, but that he had sent an army which was that moment ascending the St Lawrence for the purpose of driving the English from the country. Pontiac and his chiefs believed this story, and awaited the arrival; but, as day after day passed, he became impatient

* Parkman

and anxious to gain the tardy Canadians as allies. To accomplish this he sent out messengers inviting the principal settlers to meet him in council. At the appointed time they assembled in the Ottawa camp. Surrounding these, were numerous half-breeds, and voyageurs as repulsive as the savages themselves, and as much interested in the proceedings. After several pipes had passed around, Pontiac arose, flung a war belt at the feet of the Canadians and said:

"My brothers, how long will you suffer this bad flesh to remain upon your lands? I have told you before, and now I tell you again, that when I took up the hatchet, it was for your good. *This year the English must all perish throughout Canada.* The Master of Life commands it, and you, who know Him better than we, wish to oppose His will. Until now I have said nothing on this matter. I have not urged you to take part with us in the war. It would have been enough had you been content to sit quiet on your mats, looking on while we were fighting for you. But you have not done so. You call yourselves our friends and yet you assist the English with provision, and go about as spies among our villages. This must not continue. You must be either wholly French or wholly English. If you are French, take up that war-belt and lift the hatchet with us; but, if you are English, then we declare war upon you. We are all, alike, children of our great father, the King of France, and it is hard to fight among brethren for the sake of dogs. But, there is no choice. Look upon the belt, and let us hear your answer."

This peremptory command for the Canadians to transfer their power either to one side or the other, was most ingeniously evaded by the "Canuck" who replied. Producing a paper, he stated that it was from their father, the King of France, and commanded all his children to remain quiet, as he was coming with a large army to exterminate the English *himself.* If these orders were disobeyed the poor Canadians would be punished, while, if Pontiac made war upon them for refusing to side with him, the King would treat *him* as an enemy, and thus the unfortunate fellow would have both the French and English to contend against.

Pontiac, it is said, sat silent and mortified at this reply, but, most unexpectedly to himself one of the *bourgeois* standing on the outside of the circle, took up the war-belt, and declared that he and his companions were ready to fight for him. The chief's face was illuminated with joy and he greeted each of his new-made friends with many expressions of pleasure. The better-minded Canadians were horrified at the act of their countrymen, and the latter deemed it the best to spend the following night in the camp of their chosen comrades.

On the same evening, a party of these infamous renegades, together with a number of Indians, intrenched themselves within a short distance of the fort, for the purpose of picking off the soldiers. They were discovered as soon as it was light, and Lieutenant Hey made a charge upon them, routing all and killing two Indians. One of the latter was a nephew of the Ojibwa chief who, learning of the loss, became so enraged, that, with a party of his warriors, he ran to the house of Meloche—where Major Campbell was confined—brought the venerable and excellent man forth, tied him to the fence and shot him through and through with arrows. The body, brutally mangled, was cast into the river, and, floating ashore, was buried by the Canadians. Lieutenant M'Dougal had effected his escape, previous to this atrocious act.

In the afternoon, a man was seen running rapidly toward the fort, pursued by a number of Indians. He came up panting and exhausted. He proved to be Ensign Pauly, lately commandant at Sandusky who had taken the opportunity to escape from the embraces of the disgusting squaw who had "adopted" him.

Pontiac felt that the two schooners lying opposite the fort were a great obstacle to his success; and as his followers had tasted their mettle more than once, he now turned all his attention toward getting rid of them. It was impossible to approach them, without being discovered. His ingenuity came to the aid of his desires, and he soon devised a plan for their extermination without loss to his own warriors. It was a plan worthy of the intelligence of the chief conspirator. On the morning of the tenth of July, two boats, filled with burning pitch pine, bark and dry wood, were fastened together and sent down the stream; but, most fortunately, the current carried them by the vessel without injury. Nothing further was attempted.

But, about two o'clock on the morning of the twelfth, the sentinel saw above him a small flame, as of a candle resting upon the surface of the stream. It grew larger and more intense every moment, and soon shot forth several waving forks of fire. Then it burst forth and spread into a broad, roaring blaze that lit up the shores as if at noonday. A large mass of combustible material was burning like a furnace, sending the sparks high in air, and floating directly toward the schooner. As it passed down stream, it revealed a multitude of naked savages along the shore who watched the course of the fire raft with the most breathless interest. The masts, spars and every rope on the vessel were outlined as if drawn with ink in the luminous air, while one side was thrown into the full blaze of light, and the other shrouded in impenetrable darkness. The settlers' cabins, the palisades, the ramparts crowded with officers and men, all as silent as death, stood out in relief against the dark forest behind. The whole singular scene was awful in its sublimity.

The raft passed down between the fort and the schooner, without harming any thing. Thus a second time were the Indians baffled. Still hopeful, they made preparations to repeat the experiment. They commenced building a raft much larger than the others, and which from its great width, could be but successful. While they were employed upon this, Gladwyn was busy in erecting defenses above the two vessels, which were so formidable that the Indians, after four days' labor abandoned their scheme.

It was now the middle of summer, and Detroit had been besieged for nearly three months. Its persistent defense began to tire some of the assailing wretches. The Wyandots and Pottawatomies especially viewed the end as hardly worth the means. The former sent a deputation to Major Gladwyn asking for peace, which was at once granted. Shortly after the Pottawatomies did the same, demanding, also, that such of their numbers as were prisoners with the English should be given up. Gladwyn replied that several of his countrymen were in their hands, and must be exchanged. At this, the deputies departed and brought in but three soldiers. The commandant rebuked them severely, as he knew they had a number besides these. The deputies withdrew in a rage, but returned the next day with six prisoners. Major Gladwyn, accompanied by an officer, met the savages in the council-room. As he was on the point of giving up the Pottawatomie prisoners and concluding a treaty, one of the English prisoners called out that there were several of his companions still in the village. This broke the conference up at once. Enraged at their duplicity, Major Gladwyn ordered the deputies to depart without standing on ceremony. Observing at that instant an Ottawa warrior among them (the Ottawas were still at war), he signaled for the guard to approach and seize him. This movement saved the commandant's life, for the deputies had made the resolve that, if repulsed a second time, they would murder him and trust to fortune to make their escape from the council-house. The entrance of the soldiers prevented them from carrying out this intention, and they withdrew, sullen and furious. A few days afterward, however, they brought in all their prisoners, when peace was concluded with them.

The time wore on and little change occurred in the fortunes of the beleaguered garrison. The rattle of the tireless assailants' guns continued incessant, and the vigilance of the soldiers was not allowed to abate. The story of those days of labor and nights of pain is thus told by one of the men of the garrison, in a letter dated July 6, 1763:

"We have been besieged here two months by six hundred Indians. We have been upon the watch night and day, from the commanding officer to the lowest soldier, from the eighth of May, and have not had our clothes off, nor slept all night since it began; and shall continue so until we have a reinforcement up. We then hope to give a good account of the savages. Their camp lies about a mile and a half from the fort, and that's the nearest they choose to come now. For the first two or three days we were attacked by three or four hundred of them, but we gave them so warm a reception that they don't care for coming to see us, though they now and then get behind a house or garden and fire at us about three or four hundred yards distant. The day before yesterday we killed a chief and three others and wounded some more; yesterday went up in our sloop and battered their cabins in such a manner that they are glad to keep further off."

Another letter dated July 9th

"You have long ago heard of our gloomy situation, but the storm is blown over. Was it not very agreeable to hear every day of their cutting, carving, boiling and eating our companions? to see, every day, dead bodies floating down the river, mangled and disfigured? But Britons, you know, never shrink, we always appeared gay to spite the rascals. They boiled and eat Sir Robert Davers, and we are informed by Mr. Pauly, who escaped the other day from one of the stations surprised at the breaking out of the war, and commanded by himself, that he had seen an Indian have the skin of Captain Robertson's arm for a tobacco pouch!

"Three days ago a party of us went to demolish a breast work they had made. We finished *our* work and were returning home, but the fort, espying a party of Indians coming up as if they intended to fight, we were ordered back, made our dispositions and advanced briskly. Our front was fired upon warmly, and returned the fire for about five minutes. In the mean time, Captain Hopkins, with about twenty men, filed off to the left, *and about twenty French volunteers* filed off to the right and got between them and their fires. The villains immediately fled, and we returned, as was prudent, for a sentry whom I had placed, informed me he saw a body of them coming down from the woods, and our party, being but about eighty, was not able to cope with their united bands. In short, we beat them handsomely, and yet did not much hurt to them, for they run extremely well. We only killed their leader and wounded two others. One of them fired at me, at the distance of fifteen or twenty paces, but I suppose my terrible visage made him tremble. I think I shot him."

CHAPTER VI.

ANOTHER REINFORCEMENT FROM NIAGARA—CAPTAIN DALZELL'S ARRIVAL—HIS NIGHT EXPEDITION—ITS DISASTROUS RESULT—FURY OF THE INDIANS—A THIRD VESSEL OF RELIEF—ITS ASSAULT AND REMARKABLE PRESERVATION

WHILE affairs remained thus at Detroit, a large reinforcement, unknown to Gladwyn, had been dispatched to his relief. Captain Dalzell, with twenty two barges, containing two hundred and eighty men, several small cannon, and a good supply of provisions and ammunition, started from

Niagara. Making his way along the southern shore of Lake Erie, he halted and viewed the blackened remains of the block house of Fort Presqu'Isle, so well defended by Ensign Christie and his men. Embarking again, he reached Fort Sandusky in the latter part of July, from which he marched to the Wyandot village, burning it and destroying their cornfields.

On the twenty-ninth of July the convoy reached Detroit. When nearly opposite the fort, the Wyandots and Pottawatomies—who had just concluded a treaty of peace with Major Gladwyn—fired upon them, killing and wounding fifteen before the contest was over. The treachery of the Indians was second only to their ferocity. Gladwyn might as well have treated with hyenas.

The detachment was so large that the men had to be quartered upon the inhabitants. Among them were twenty rangers, commanded by Major Rogers, regular bush fighters, ever ready for an affray. Their arrival, it may well be supposed, occasioned a season of rejoicing with the garrison, saddened, however, by the death of several under their own eyes, from the hands of the faithless Wyandots and Pottawatomies.

Major Gladwyn and Captain Dalzell immediately held a conference. Dalzell stated that, in his opinion, the time had arrived to strike a death blow at the ambition of Pontiac, and he asked permission to march out upon the following night and attack the Indians in their camp. Gladwyn, who was so well acquainted with the strength and resources of the chief, at first was unwilling, but the lion hearted Captain would hear no refusal, and was so urgent and strenuous that the commandant at length yielded.*

On the thirtieth of July orders were issued and preparations made for the attack. With an unpardonable want of discretion, some of the officers allowed several Canadians to know their intentions, one of whom betrayed it all to Pontiac, who, as may be expected, made every thing ready to receive the assailants. At two o'clock in the morning, two hundred and fifty soldiers, two deep, passed noiselessly through the

* This is the same Dalzell who was a joint hero with Israel Putnam in many of his most memorable adventures.

gates and marched up the left river-bank Two large *batteaux*, each containing a swivel, kept abreast of them in the river The advanced guard of twenty five was led by Lieutenant Brown, the center by Captain Gray, and the rear by Captain Grant ' The night was still, close and sultry, and the men marched in light undress. On their right was the dark, gleaming surface of the river, with a margin of sand intervening, on their left a succession of Canadian houses, with barns, orchards and corn-fields, from whence the clamorous barking of watch-dogs saluted them as they passed The inhabitants, roused from sleep, looked from the windows in astonishment and alarm An old man has told the writer how, when a child, he climbed on the roof of his father's house, to look down on the glimmering bayonets, and how, long after the troops had passed, their heavy and measured tramp sounded from afar through the still night. Thus the English moved forward to the attack, little thinking that, behind houses and inclosures, Indian scouts watched every yard of their progress—little suspecting that Pontiac, apprised by the Canadians of their plan, had broken up his camp, and was coming against them with all his warriors, armed and decorated for battle."*

Referring to the map, the reader will notice a small stream, which puts in from the northern shore, a short distance above Detroit At the point where the bridge is marked, the stream descends through a deep and wild-looking hollow, while upon the opposite side the river-bank rises in several ridges. Here Pontiac had erected several intrenchments, besides throwing together several piles of cord wood further on Behind these were crouching hundreds of Indians, who, with guns ready cocked, listened to the dull tramp of the approaching soldiers

The advanced guard had crossed the bridge, and the main body was just entering, when loud yells burst forth, and a sheet of fire flamed along the whole ridge, like the broadside of a frigate. One-half the advanced guard fell dead, and the others recoiled in terror, but Dalzell, in his clear, stirring voice, inspired his men with his own courage Advancing to the front he led them to the attack A second volley was poured into them, when, furious with rage, he led the men on

* Parkman, Life of Pontiac

a rapid run across the bridge and up the ridge, but not an Indian was visible. Half frantic with fear and fury the soldiers charged behind the fence and the intrenchments, but the agile savages were gone. The night had now become of inky darkness, and the men were soon scattered and lost among the houses and inclosures. The only resource left was to retreat and wait for daylight. Accordingly, Captain Grant led his men across the bridge where the others soon followed, with the exception of a small party which remained to check the rapid pursuit of the enemy. Amid a hot firing upon both sides, the dead and wounded were placed in the two batteaux. Immediately after, the rapid report of musketry was heard in the rear, where Captain Grant was stationed. The shots had come from the house of Meloche and the surrounding orchards, where large numbers of savages had intrenched themselves. Captain Grant charged right at them, driving them at the point of the bayonet from the orchard and from the house where they found two Canadians, who stated that the Indians had gone in great numbers to occupy the houses below, from which they intended to cut off their retreat.

This being the case, the only hope was in instant retreat. The men were collected in marching order and the march commenced, Captain Grant leading and Dalzell bringing up the rear. Numbers of Indians dogged them, and when their fire became too galling, the soldiers wheeled and returned it. In this manner they proceeded for over a half-mile, when they came abreast of a number of barns protected by strong pickets. These were safely passed by the advance party, but, when the center and rear came opposite, loud yells greeted them, and a most murderous volley was poured into their ranks. The men shrunk, hesitated and recoiled, and had it not been for Dalzell would have broke and fled. Though severely wounded himself, he commanded, threatened, and, it is said, smote several timid ones with the flat of his sword. His persistent efforts partially restored the men, when the fire was returned with considerable effect.

It was now near daybreak, and the incessant rattle of rifles together with the horrid yells of the Indian, so drowned the voices of the leaders that their commands could not be heard. The soldiers read their orders only in the excited faces and frenzied gestures. One of the houses had been filled by the savages and from its windows scores of rifles were continually flashing. Major Rogers at the head of his rangers split open the door with an axe and burst in among them like a thunderbolt. They fled in every direction, as the rangers swarmed in. At the same instant Captain Gray was sent to dislodge a number that were firing from behind the fences. He charged them at the head of his company, but fell with a mortal wound before he reached them. His men kept on and routed the Indians. The retreat was now resumed with comparatively good order. The fire of the Indians had nearly ceased, but, leaping forward they seized the stragglers, cut them down and scalped them without mercy. A poor Sergeant of the 55th, so wounded that he could not walk, raised himself on his hands and gazed after his retreating comrades with such a despairing, beseeching expression, that the noble-hearted Dalzell, now wounded himself in two places, ran toward him with the intention of rescuing the man from his inhuman enemies. As he reached out his arms to seize the wounded soldier, a shot struck him and he fell dead before him. None paused to see their fate. There was no time. Death was hanging on their rear.

The Indians were rapidly concentrating their numbers again, and the massacre would have been far more dreadful had not Rogers with his rangers taken possession of another house, which commanded the road and protected the retreat.

The account of this battle by Parkman is so graphic and truthful that we transcribe that portion descriptive of the remaining part of the fight:—

"Rogers entered this house with some of his men, while many panic-stricken regulars broke in after him, in their eagerness to gain a temporary shelter. The house was a large and strong one, and the women of the neighborhood had crowded into the cellar for refuge. While some of the soldiers looked in blind terror for a place of concealment, others seized upon a keg of whisky in one of the rooms, and quaffed the liquor with eager thirst, while others, again, piled packs of furs, furniture, and all else within their reach, against the windows, to serve as a barricade. Panting and breathless, their faces moist with sweat and blackened with gunpowder, they thrust their muskets through the openings, and fired out upon the whooping assailants. At intervals a bullet flew whizzing through a crevice, striking down a man, perchance, or rapping harmlessly against the partitions. Old Campau, the master of the house, stood on a trap-door to prevent the frightened soldiers from seeking shelter among the women in the cellar. A ball grazed his gray head, and buried itself in the wall, where a few years since it might still have been seen. The screams of the half-stifled women below, the quavering war-whoops without, the shouts and curses of the soldiers, the groans and blaspheming of the wounded men, mingled in a scene of clamorous confusion, and it was long before the authority of Rogers could restore order.

"In the mean time, Captain Grant, with his advance party, had moved forward about half a mile, when he found some orchards and inclosures, by means of which he could maintain himself until the center and rear should arrive. From this point he detached all the men he could spare to occupy the houses below; and as soldiers soon began to come in from the rear, he was enabled to reinforce these detachments, until a complete line of communication was established with the fort and the retreat effectually secured. Within an hour the whole party had arrived, with the exception of Rogers and his men, who were quite unable to come off, being besieged in the house of Campau, by full two hundred Indians. The two armed batteaux had gone down to the fort, laden with the dead and wounded. They now returned, and, in obedience to an order from Captain Grant, proceeded up the river to a point opposite Campau's house, where they opened a fire of swivels, which swept the ground above and below it, and completely scattered the assailants. Rogers and his party now came out and marched down the road, to unite themselves with Grant. The two batteaux accompanied them closely, and by a constant fire, restrained the Indians from making an attack. Scarcely had Rogers left the house at one door, when the enemy entered it at another, to obtain the scalps from two or three corpses left behind. Foremost of them all, a withered old squaw rushed in, with a shrill scream, and slashing open one of the dead bodies with her knife, scooped up the blood between her hands, and quaffed it with a ferocious ecstasy."

The retreat was conducted so admirably by Captain Grant, that not another of his men was injured. At eight o'clock in the morning the last man of the decimated detachment was received within the walls of the fort, when it was found that fifty-nine had been killed and wounded. [The Indians had not lost more than one fourth that number,* it was afterward ascertained.]

The death of the noble Dalzell and so many of his brave

* Some authorities give the loss of the English as seventy besides forty wounded.

men spread a gloom for the time over Detroit. All felt that, had not the Canadians proved traitors, the Indians would have been most completely punished. The condition of the garrison, however, was now much better than it had ever been. There were over three hundred men within the inclosure, every one of whom had had abundant experience in Indian warfare. These were well provided with ammunition and provisions, and Gladwyn felt that the raising of the siege was only a question of time and perhaps of *eternity* with a few more of his brave fellows.

Pontiac was so overjoyed with his success that he sent his runners for hundreds of miles through the adjoining country with news of the battle. Vast numbers came from great distances to join him, until over a thousand were dancing and yelling in his village, and he became stronger in his belief that the garrison would eventually fall into his hands. The vision of vengeance which haunted him seemed to demonize all around him.

Now comes a comparatively long season of quiet for Detroit. It is true the Indians still hovered around it, but few opportunities were given for any trial of strength or stratagem between the two forces. Now and then a man was shot, or an over-eager Indian picked off; but nothing worth relating occurred until the fourth of September, when perhaps the most remarkable incident of this remarkable siege took place.

The smaller of the two schooners had been sent to Niagara with letters and dispatches. She was now returning with a crew of twelve men, including the captain and mate, besides six Mohawk Indians who professed friendship with the English. On the morning in question the vessel entered Detroit river, when these savages asked permission to go ashore. The captain, with great indiscretion, gave them permission, and they took their departure. The schooner held her course up the river until evening, when the wind dying away, she anchored off Fighting Island.

She was now near the spot where the other had been attacked, and the absence of the Mohawks filled the crew with such apprehension that not one went below. All remained on deck, threading it with stealthy tread or, leaning over the bulwarks, strained their eyes to pierce the Stygian gloom. Every sound on shore sent a thrill of fear through the watchers. The call of the night hawk or whippowil was to them the signals of their insidious enemies. They indeed had good reason to watch and fear; for three hundred and fifty Indians—about thirty times their own number—were at that moment gliding over the water for their sacrifice. It was not until their canoes shot under the bows of the vessel that they were seen. A cannon was hastily directed and discharged among them, and the next minute, holding their knives in their teeth, they were clambering up the sides of the vessel by hundreds. The crew fired their guns among them, and then catching up spears and hatchets, met them with the fury of madmen as they dropped upon the deck. Knowing no quarter was to be expected they resolved to die fighting, and so desperately did they exert themselves that, in a few moments, they had killed and wounded nearly th y. But, even this destruction could not roll back the living stream pouring over the bulwarks. The captain was killed and several of his crew disabled so that scarce a half-dozen remained

"BLOW UP THE VESSEL!" commanded the mate, seeing that all hope was gone. These words were understood by several Wyandots, who communicated their meaning to the others, and the next second every Indian had leaped overboard, and were swimming away with all their strength to escape the dire explosion. Not an enemy remained on board the schooner, and not one showed himself during the night.

Two of the crew were killed, and four badly wounded. The remaining six were unharmed. It was afterward ascertained that eight of the Indians subsequently died from their wounds. The next morning the schooner set sail and passed safely up to the fort. For the conduct of the men on this occasion, the Commander in Chief ordered a medal to be struck and presented to each

CHAPTER VII

THE FALL OF MACKINAW AND ADVENTURES OF AN ENGLISH TRADER

The only authentic account of the fall of Mackinaw, is that given by Henry, an English trader, who was in the fort at the time, and participated in the calamities. This account was published in 1809, in New York, and has been preserved by Mr Schoolcraft, in his interesting volumes.

"When I reached Mackinaw," says he, "I found several other traders, who had arrived before me, from different parts of the country, and who, in general, declared the disposition of the Indians to be hostile to the English, and even apprehended some attack. M. Laurent Ducharme distinctly informed Major Etherington that a plan was absolutely conceived for destroying him, his garrison, and all the English in the upper country; but the commandant, believing this and other reports to be without foundation, proceeding only from idle or ill disposed persons, and of a tendency to do mischief, expressed much displeasure against M. Ducharme, and threatened to send the next person who should bring a story of the same kind a prisoner to Detroit.

"The garrison, at this time, consisted of ninety privates, two subalterns, and the commandant, and the English merchants at the fort were four in number. Thus strong, few entertained anxiety concerning the Indians, who had no weapons but small arms.

"Meanwhile, the Indians, from every quarter, were daily assembling in unusual numbers, but with every appearance of friendship; frequenting the fort, and disposing of their peltries in such a manner as to dissipate almost every one's fears. For myself, on one occasion, I took the liberty of observing to Major Etherington that, in my judgment, no confidence ought to be placed in them, and that I was informed no less than four hundred lay around the fort.

"In return, the Major only rallied me on my timidity; and it is to be confessed, that if this officer neglected admonition on his part, so did I on mine. Shortly after my first arrival at Mackinaw, in the preceding year, a Chippewa, named Wawatam, began to come frequently to my house, betraying in his demeanor strong personal regard. After this had continued some time, he came, on a certain day, bringing with him his whole family, and, at the same time, a large present, consisting of skins, sugar, and dried meat. Having laid these in a heap, he commenced a speech, in which he informed me that, some years before, he had observed a fast, devoting himself, according to the custom of his nation, to solitude, and to the mortification of his body, in the hope to obtain, from the Great Spirit, protection through all his days; that on this occasion he had dreamed of adopting an Englishman as his son, brother, and friend; that, from the moment in which he first beheld me, he had recognized me as the person whom the Great Spirit had been pleased to point out to him for a brother; that he hoped that I would not refuse his present; and that he should forever regard me as one of his family.

"I could not do otherwise than accept the present, and declare my willingness to have so good a man as this appeared to be for my friend and brother. I offered a present in return for that which I had received, which Wawatam accepted; and then, thanking me for the favor which he said that I had rendered him, he left me, and soon after set out on his winter's hunt.

"Twelve months had now elapsed since the occurrence of this incident, and I had almost forgot the person of my *brother*, when, on the second day of June, Wawatam came again to my house, in a temper of mind visibly melancholy and thoughtful. He told me that he had just returned from his *wintering-ground*, and I asked after his health; but without answering my question, he went on to say that he was sorry to find me returned from the Sault; that he intended to proceed to that place himself, immediately after his arrival at Mackinaw; and that he wished me to go there along with him and his family the next morning. To all this he joined an inquiry, whether or not the commandant had heard bad news, adding that during the winter he had himself been frequently disturbed with the *noise of evil birds,* and further suggesting that there were numerous Indians near the fort, many of whom had never shown themselves within it. Wawatam was about forty-five years of age, of an excellent character among his nation, and a chief.

"Referring much of what he had heard to the peculiarities of the Indian character, I did not pay all the attention which they will be found to have deserved to the entreaties and remarks of my visitor. I answered that I could not think of going to the Sault as soon as the next morning, but would follow him there after the arrival of my clerks. Finding himself unable to prevail with me, he withdrew for the day, but early the next morning he came again, bringing with him his wife, and a present of dried meat. At this interview, after stating that he had several packs of beaver for which he intended to deal with me, he expressed a second time his apprehensions, from the numerous Indians who were around the fort, and earnestly pressed me to consent to an immediate departure for the Sault. As a reason for this particular request, he assured me that all the Indians proposed to come in a body, that day, to the fort, to demand liquor of the commandant, and that he wished me to be gone before they should grow intoxicated.

"I had made, at the period to which I am now referring, so much progress in the language in which Wawatam addressed me, as to be able to hold an ordinary conversation in it; but the Indian manner of speech is so extravagantly figurative, that it is only for a perfect master to follow and comprehend it entirely. Had I been further advanced in this respect, I think that I should have gathered so much information from this, my friendly monitor, as would put me in possession of the designs of the enemy, and enabled me to save, as well others as myself. As it was, I unfortunately turned a deaf ear to every thing, leaving Wawatam and his wife, after long and patient, but ineffectual efforts, to depart alone, with dejected countenances, and not before they had each let fall some tears.

"In the course of the same day, I observed that the Indians came in great numbers into the fort, purchasing tomahawks—small axes of one pound weight—and frequently desiring to see silver arm-bands, and other valuable ornaments of which I had a large quantity for sale. The ornaments, however, they in no instance purchased, but, after turning them over, left them, saying they would call again next day. Their motive, as it afterward appeared, was no other than the artful one of discovering, by requesting to see them, the particular place of their deposit, so that they might lay their hands on them in the moment of pillage, with the greater certainty and dispatch

"At night I turned in my mind the visits of Wawatam, but, though they were calculated to excite uneasiness, nothing induced me to believe that serious mischief was at hand

"The following day, being the fourth of June, was the King's birthday A Chippewa came to tell me that his nation was going to play at *baggatiway* with the Sacs or Saukies, another Indian nation, for a high wager He invited me to witness the sport, adding that the commandant was to be there, and would bet on the side of the Chippewas. In consequence of this information, I went to the commandant, and expostulated with him a little, representing that the Indians might possibly have some sinister end in view, but the commandant only smiled at my suspicions.

"*Baggatiway*, called by the Canadians *le jeu de la crosse*, is played with a bat and ball The bat is about four feet in length, curved, and terminating in a sort of racket Two posts are planted in the ground, at a considerable distance from each other, as a mile or more Each party has its post, and the game consists in throwing the ball up to the post of the adversary The ball at the beginning is placed in the middle of the course, and each party endeavors as well to throw the ball out of the direction of its own post, as into that of the adversary's

"I did not go myself to see the match which was now to be played without the fort, because there being a canoe prepared to depart, on the following day, for Montreal, I employed myself in writing letters to my friends, and even when a fellow trader, Mr Tracy, happened to call upon me, saying that another canoe had just arrived from Detroit, and proposing that I should go with him to the beach, to inquire the news, it so happened that I still remained to finish my letters, promising to follow Mr Tracy in the course of a few minutes Mr Tracy had not gone more than twenty paces from the door, when I heard an Indian war-cry, and a noise of general confusion.

"Going instantly to my window, I saw a crowd of Indians within the fort, furiously cutting down and scalping every Englishman they found. In particular, I witnessed the fate of Lieutenant Jemette.

"I had, in the room in which I was, a fowling piece, loaded with swan shot. This I immediately seized, and held it for a few minutes, waiting to hear the drum beat to arms. In this dreadful interval I saw several of my countrymen fall, and more than one struggling between the knees of an Indian, who, holding him in this manner, scalped him while yet alive.

"At length, disappointed in the hope of resistance made to the enemy, and sensible, of course, that no effort of my own unassisted arm could avail against four hundred Indians, I thought only of seeking shelter. Amid the slaughter which was raging, I observed many of the Canadian inhabitants of the fort calmly looking on, neither opposing the Indians nor suffering injury; and from this circumstance I conceived a hope of finding a place of security in their houses.

"Between the yard-door of my own house and that of M. Langlade, my next neighbor, there was only a low fence, over which I easily climbed. At my entrance, I found the whole family at the windows, gazing at the scene of blood before them. I addressed myself immediately to Langlade, begging that he would put me in some place of safety, till the heat of the affair should be over—an act of charity by which he might perhaps preserve me from the general massacre; but, while I uttered my petition, M. Langlade, who had looked for a moment at me, turned again to the window, shrugging his shoulders, and intimating that he could do nothing for me. ' *Que voudriez-vous que j'en ferais?*'

"This was a moment for despair; but the next, a Pani woman,* a slave of M. Langlade's, beckoned to me to follow her. She brought me to a door, which she opened, desiring me to enter, and telling me that it led to the garret, where I must go and conceal myself. I joyfully obeyed her directions; and she, having followed me up to the garret door, locked it after me, and, with great presence of mind, took away the key

* The Panies are an Indian nation of the South

"This shelter obtained, if shelter I could hope to find it, I was naturally anxious to know what might still be passing without. Through an aperture, which afforded me a view of the area of the fort, I beheld, in shapes the foulest and most terrible, the ferocious triumphs of barbarian conquerors. The dead were scalped and mangled, the dying were writhing and shrieking under the unsatiated knife and tomahawk, and from the bodies of some, ripped open, their savage butchers were drinking the blood, scooped up in the hollow of joined hands, and quaffed amid shouts of rage and victory. I was shaken not only with horror, but with fear. The sufferings which I witnessed, I seemed on the point of experiencing. No long time elapsed before—every one being destroyed who could be found—there was a general cry of 'All is finished!' At the same instant, I heard some of the Indians enter the house in which I was * * * *

"The door was unlocked and opened, and the Indians ascending the stairs, before I had completely crept into a small opening which presented itself at one end of the heap. An instant after, four Indians entered the room, all armed with tomahawks, and all besmeared with blood upon every part of their bodies.

"The die appeared to be cast. I could scarcely breathe, but I thought the throbbing of my heart occasioned a noise loud enough to betray me. The Indians walked in every direction about the garret, and one of them approached me so closely that at a particular moment, had he put forth his hand, he must have touched me. Still I remained undiscovered, a circumstance to which the dark color of my clothes, and the want of light in the room, which had no window, and in the corner in which I was, must have contributed. In a word, after taking several turns in the room, during which they told M. Langlade how many they had killed, and how many scalps they had taken, they returned down stairs, and I, with sensations not to be expressed, heard the door, which was the barrier between me and my fate, locked for the second time.

"There was a feather bed on the floor, and on this, exhausted as I was by the agitation of my mind, I threw myself down and fell asleep. In this state I remained till the dusk of the evening, when I was awakened by the second opening of the door. The person that now entered was M Langlade's wife, who was much surprised at finding me, but advised me not to be uneasy, observing that the Indians had killed most of the English, but that she hoped I might myself escape. A shower of rain having begun to fall, she had come to stop a hole in the roof. On her going away, I begged her to send me a little water to drink, which she did.

"As night was now advancing, I continued to lie on the bed, ruminating on my condition, but unable to discover a resource from which I could hope for life. A flight to Detroit had no probable chance of success. The distance from Mackinaw was four hundred miles, I was without provisions, and the whole length of the road lay through Indian countries—countries of an enemy in arms, where the first man whom I should meet would kill me. To stay where I was threatened the same issue. As before, fatigue of mind, and not tranquillity, suspended my cares, and procured me further sleep.

"The game of *baggatiway*, as from the description above given, will have been perceived, is necessarily attended with much violence and noise. In the ardor of contest, the ball, as has been suggested, if it can not be thrown to the goal desired, is struck in any direction by which it can be diverted from that designed by the adversary. At such a moment, therefore, nothing could be less liable to excite premature alarm, than that the ball should be tossed over the pickets of the fort, nor that, having fallen there, it should be followed on the instant by all engaged in the game, as well the one party as the other, all eager, all struggling, all shouting, all in the unrestrained pursuit of a rude, athletic exercise. Nothing could be less fitted to excite premature alarm, nothing, therefore, could be more happily devised, under the circumstances, than a stratagem like this; and this was, in fact, the stratagem which the Indians had employed, by which they had obtained possession of the fort, and by which they had been enabled to slaughter and subdue its garrison, and such of its other inhabitants as they pleased. To be still more certain of success, they had prevailed upon as many as they could, by a pretext the least liable to suspicion, to come voluntarily without the pickets, and particularly the commandant and garrison themselves.

"The respite which sleep afforded me, during the night, was put an end to by the return of morning. I was again on the rack of apprehension. At sunrise, I heard the family stirring, and presently after, Indian voices, informing M Langlade that they had not found my hapless self among the dead, and they supposed me to be somewhere concealed. M. Langdale appeared, from what followed, to be by this time acquainted with the place of my retreat, of which, no doubt, he had been informed by his wife. The poor woman, as soon as the Indians mentioned me, declared to her husband, in the French tongue, that he should no longer keep me in his house, but deliver me up to my pursuers, giving as a reason for this measure, that should the Indians discover his instrumentality in my concealment, they might revenge it on her children, and that it was better that I should die than they. M Langlade resisted, at first, this sentence of his wife's, but soon suffered her to prevail, informing the Indians that he had been told I was in his house, that I had come there without his knowledge, and that he would put me into their hands. This was no sooner expressed than he began to ascend the stairs, the Indians following upon his heels

"I now resigned myself to the fate with which I was menaced, and regarding every attempt at concealment as vain, I arose from the bed, and presented myself full in view to the Indians who were entering the room. They were all in a state of intoxication, and entirely naked, except about the middle. One of them, named Wenniway, whom I had previously known, and who was upward of six feet in height, had his entire face and body covered with charcoal and grease, only that a spot of white, of two inches in diameter, encircled either eye. This man walked up to me, seized me with one hand by the collar of the coat, while in the other he held a large carving knife, as if to plunge it in my breast, his eyes, meanwhile, were fixed steadfastly on mine. At length, after some seconds of the most anxious suspense, he dropped his arm, saying 'I won't kill you!' To this he added, that he had frequently engaged in wars against the English, and had brought away many scalps; that on a certain occasion he had lost a brother, whose name was Musinigon, and that I should be called after him

"A reprieve upon any terms placed me among the living, and gave me back the sustaining voice of hope; but Wenniway ordered me down stairs, and there informed me that I was to be taken to his cabin, where, and indeed everywhere else, the Indians were all mad with liquor. Death again was threatened, and not as possible only, but as certain. I mentioned my fears on this subject to M. Langlade, begging him to represent the danger to my master. M. Langlade, in this instance, did not withhold his compassion, and Wenniway immediately consented that I should remain where I was, till he found another opportunity to take me away.

"Thus far secure, I reascended my garret-stairs, in order to place myself the furthest possible out of the reach of insult from drunken Indians; but I had not remained there more than an hour, when I was called to the room below, in which was an Indian, who said that I must go with him out of the fort, Wenniway having sent him to fetch me. This man, as well as Wenniway himself, I had seen before. In the preceding year, I had allowed him to take on credit, for which he was still in my debt, and a short time previous to the surprise of the fort, he had said, upon my upbraiding him with his dishonesty, that 'he would pay me before long!' This speech now came fresh into my memory, and led me to suspect that the fellow had formed a design against my life. I communicated the suspicion to M. Langlade, but he gave for answer that 'I was not my own master, and I must do as I was ordered.'

"The Indian, on his part, directed that before I left the house I should undress myself, declaring that my coat and shirt became him better than it did me. His pleasure, in this respect, being complied with, there was no other alternative left me than either to go out naked, or put on the clothes of the Indian, which he freely gave me in exchange. His motive for thus stripping me of my own apparel was no other, as I afterward learned, than this—that it might not be stained with blood when he should kill me.

"I was now told to proceed, and my driver followed me close, till I had passed the gate of the fort, when I turned toward the spot where I knew the Indians to be encamped. This, however, did not suit the purpose of my enemy, who seized me by the arm, and drew me violently in the opposite direction, to the distance of fifty yards above the fort. Here, finding that I was approaching the bushes and sand-hills, I determined to proceed no further, but told the Indian that I believed he meant to murder me, and, if so, he might as well strike where I was as at any greater distance. He replied, with coolness, that my suspicions were just, and that he meant to pay me in this manner for my goods. At the same time, he produced a knife, and held me in a position to receive the intended blow. Both this and that which followed were necessarily the affair of a moment. By some effort, too sudden and too little dependent on thought to be explained or remembered, I was enabled to arrest his arm, and give him a sudden push, by which I turned him from me, and released myself from his grasp. This was no sooner done than I ran toward the fort, with all the swiftness in my power, the Indian following me, and I expecting every moment to feel his knife. I succeeded in my flight, and, on entering the fort, I saw Wenniway standing in the midst of the area, and to him I hastened for protection. Wenniway desired the Indian to desist; but the latter pursued me around him, making several strokes at me with his knife, and foaming at the mouth with rage at the repeated failure of his purpose. At length Wenniway drew near to M. Langlade's house, and, the door being open, I ran into it. The Indian followed me, but, on my entering the house, he voluntarily abandoned the pursuit.

"Preserved so often and so unexpectedly, as it had now been my lot to be, I returned to my garret, with a strong inclination to believe that, through the will of an overruling Power, no Indian enemy could do me hurt; but new trials, as I believed, were at hand, when, at ten o'clock in the evening, I was roused from sleep, and once more desired to descend the stairs. Not less, however, to my satisfaction than surprise, I was summoned only to meet Major Etherington, Mr. Bostwick, and Lieutenant Lesslie, who were in the room below.

"These gentlemen had been taken prisoners while looking at the game without the fort, and immediately stripped of all their clothes. They were now sent into the fort, under the charge of Canadians, because, the Indians having resolved on getting drunk, the chiefs were apprehensive that they would be murdered if they continued in the camp. Lieutenant Jemette and seventy soldiers had been killed, and but twenty Englishmen, including soldiers, were still alive. These were all within the fort, together with nearly three hundred Canadians belonging to the canoes, etc.

"These being our numbers, myself and others proposed to Major Etherington to make an effort for regaining possession of the fort, and maintaining it against the Indians. The Jesuit missionary was consulted on the project, but he discouraged us by his representations, not only of the merciless treatment which we must expect from the Indians, should they regain their superiority, but of the little dependence which was to be placed upon our Canadian auxiliaries. Thus the fort and prisoners remained in the hands of the Indians, though, through the whole night, the prisoners and whites were in actual possession, and they were without the gates.

"That whole night, or the greater part of it, was passed in mutual condolence, and my fellow-prisoners shared my garret. In the morning, being again called down, I found my master, Wenniway, and was desired to follow him. He led me to a small house within the fort, where, in a narrow room, and almost dark, I found Ezekiel Solomons, an Englishman from Detroit, and a soldier, all prisoners. With these I remained in painful suspense, as to the scene that was next to present itself, till ten o'clock in the forenoon, when an Indian arrived, and marched us to the lake side, where a canoe appeared ready for departure, and in which we found that we were to embark.

"Our voyage, full of doubt as it was, would have commenced immediately, but that one of the Indians who was to be of the party was absent. His arrival was to be waited for and this occasioned a very long delay, during which we were exposed to a very keen north east wind. An old shirt was all that covered me, I suffered much from the cold, and in this extremity, M. Langlade coming down to the beach, I asked him for a blanket, promising, if I lived, to pay him for it, at any price he pleased; but the answer I received was this, that he could let me have no blanket unless there were some one to be security for the payment. For myself, he observed, I had no longer any property in that country. I had no more to say to M. Langlade, but presently, seeing another Canadian, named John Cuchrise, I addressed to him a similar request, and was not refused. Naked as I was, and rigorous as was the weather, but for the blanket I must have perished. At noon our party was all collected, the prisoners all embarked, and we steered for the Isles du Castor—Beaver Island—in Lake Michigan.

"The soldier who was our companion in misfortune was made fast to a bar of the canoe by a rope tied round his neck, as is the manner of the Indians in transporting their prisoners. The rest were left unconfined; but a paddle was put into each of our hands, and we were made to use it. The Indians in the canoe were seven in number, the prisoners four. I had left, as will be recollected, Major Etherington, Lieutenant Lesslie, and Mr. Bostwick at M. Langlade's, and was now joined in misery with Mr. Ezekiel Solomons, the soldier, and the Englishman who had newly arrived from Detroit. This was on the sixth day of June. The fort was taken on the fourth; I surrendered myself to Wenniway on the fifth; and this was the third day of our distress.

"We were bound, as I have said, for Isles du Castor, which lie in the mouth of Lake Michigan, and we should have crossed the lake, but that a thick fog came on, on account of which the Indians deemed it safer to keep the shore close under their lee. We, therefore, approached the lands of the Ottawas, and their village of L'Arbre Croche, which village is situated about twenty miles to the westward of Mickinaw, on the opposite side of the tongue of land on which the fort is built.

"Every half-hour the Indians gave their war-whoop, one for every prisoner in their canoe. This is a general custom, by the aid of which all other Indians, within hearing, are apprised of the number of prisoners they are carrying.

"In this manner we reached Wagoshense, Fox Point—a long point, stretching westward into the lake, and which the Ottawas make a carrying place, so as to avoid going round it. It is distant eighteen miles from Mickinaw. After the Indians had made their war whoop as before, an Ottawa appeared upon the beach, who made signs that we should land. In consequence, we approached. The Ottawa asked the news, and kept the Chippewas in further conversation, till we were within a few yards of the land, and in shallow water. At this moment a hundred men rushed upon us, from among the bushes, and dragged all the prisoners out of the canoe, amid a terrifying shout.

"We now believed that our last suffering was approaching; but no sooner were we fairly on shore, and on our legs, than the chiefs of the party advanced and gave each of us their hands, telling us that they were our friends, the Ottawas, whom the Chippewas had insulted, by destroying the English without consulting with them on the affair. They added, that what they had done was for the purpose of saving our lives, the Chippewas having been carrying us to the Isles du Castor, only to kill and devour us.

"The reader's imagination is here distracted by the variety of our fortunes, and he may well paint to himself the state of mind of those who sustained them, who were the sport or the victims of a series of events, more like dreams than realities, more like fiction than truth. It was not long before we embarked again, in the canoes of the Ottawas, who, the same evening, relanded us at Mackinaw, where they marched us into the fort, in view of the Chippewas, confounded at beholding the Ottawas espousing a side opposite to their own.

"The Ottawas, who had accompanied us in sufficient numbers, took possession of the fort. We, who had changed, but were still prisoners, were lodged in the house of the commandant, and strictly guarded."

Early the next morning, a general council was held, in which the Chippewas complained much of the conduct of the Ottawas, in robbing them of their prisoners; alleging that all the Indians—the Ottawas alone excepted—were at war with the English, that Pontiac had taken Detroit, that the king of France had awoke, and repossessed himself of Quebec and Montreal; and that the English were meeting destruction not only at Mackinaw, but in every other part of the world. From all this, they inferred that it became the Ottawas to restore their prisoners, and to join in the war; and the speech was followed by large presents, being part of the plunder of the fort, and which was previously heaped in the center of the room. The Indians rarely make their answer till the day after they have heard the arguments offered.

In the morning Henry and his companions were handed over to the Chippewas, the Ottawas assuring them that their owners intended to kill and *make a broth of them*. They were marched into the Chippewa village and put into a lodge where fourteen prisoners were already confined. Each, with the exception of Henry, had a rope around his neck, and were tied to a pole, the supporter of the building. The night was a sleepless one to Henry. He had been deprived of his blanket, and had not tasted food for two days. He was offered a piece of bread cut from a loaf, with a knife besmeared with the blood of his countrymen, and spit upon by the savages.

At noon, the Indian Wawatam, whom Henry mentions as his friend, visited the Chippewa chief. He made a speech, claiming the trader as his adopted brother, and offering a large ransom for him. Menehwehna accepted the offer, and the hero of so many adventures accompanied Wawatam to his lodge, where he was clothed, fed, and treated indeed as a brother.

The next day Henry saw the dead bodies of seven of his companions dragged forth, all slain by Le Grand Sable, a chief who had been absent at the time of the massacre, and who took this occasion to show his approval of what had been done. Of the English traders who fell into the hands of the Indians at the fall of Mackinaw, Mr Tracy only lost his life. Bostwick and Solomons were taken by the Ottawas and after the peace taken to Montreal, where they were ransomed. Of ninety troops about seventy were killed; the others were also ransomed after the war had ended.

Wawatam proved a faithful friend. He protected Henry against the fury of his companions, saving his life time and again. They spent the winter hunting together, along the river Aux Sables, and returned to Mackinaw in May, where, after a time, Henry found opportunity to escape and reach the English settlements.

CHAPTER VIII.

THE INDIANS ASK FOR PEACE—PONTIAC LEAVES DETROIT FOR THE MAUMEE—ENGLISH ARMIES ORDERED INTO THE COUNTRY—BRADSTREET'S AND BOUQUET'S EXPEDITIONS—A PEACE CONQUERED

DETROIT was besieged in May. October found it in the same condition. The garrison was on short allowance, while many of the Indians also felt the need of provisions. Compelled to depart to their hunting grounds, they concluded to make peace with Major Gladwyn, hoping by a mere pretext to remain unmolested during the winter. In the spring they would be doubly prepared to renew the war. Their ferocious desire for blood would impel them to any perfidy to gain time. Accordingly, the chief of one of the branches of the Ojibwas visited the fort and made a speech to Gladwyn, commencing with the infamous falsehood that he and his followers always had been friends of the English. He said he wished to make a lasting peace with them, and added that the Wyandots, Pottawatomies and Ojibwas had instructed him to say they were sorry for what they had done and begged for forgiveness. The commandant saw through these transparent falsehoods, but he deemed it best to listen to them. He replied that although he did not possess the power to make peace, yet he would grant a truce with them.

This was a good stroke of policy for Gladwyn. His men were nearly famished, and, by making the truce, he was given an opportunity to collect provisions. So well did he improve the occasion, that, in a short time, he was furnished with enough to last the winter.

The death-blow to Pontiac's hopes of the capture of Detroit was given, on the thirtieth of October. On that day he was visited by several French messengers, who brought a letter from M. Neyon, principal French commandant in the Illinois country. This letter advised Pontiac to cease his hostilities to the English, telling him he need expect no assistance from the French, as they and the English were at peace, and regarded each other as brothers.

This letter rendered Pontiac furious. He saw that he had

been deluded with false hopes by the Canadians, and that nothing but his own resources were left to depend upon. Collecting a number of his chiefs, he left Detroit for Maumee river, vowing vengeance, and resolved to stir up the Indians in that section. No tiger baffled of its prey ever felt less desire for peace.

As the winter advanced, the Indians gradually withdrew from the vicinity of Detroit, until the surrounding woods were nearly deserted. Still, the garrison by no means felt safe. A letter dated December 3, 1763, says: "'Tis said that Pontiac and his tribe have gone to the Mississippi, but we don't believe it." And even as late as March 25th, 1764—nearly a year from the commencement of the siege—an officer writes: "About twelve days ago, several scalping-parties of the Pottawatomies came to the settlement, etc. We now sleep in our clothes, expecting an alarm every night!"

It was now that the influence of Sir William Johnson was felt. Indeed, so conspicuous had his services already become, that, in the summary of news from the American colonies, given at intervals in the old *Gentleman's Magazine*, his doings frequently comprehended the greater portion.

The Six Nations, with the exception of the Senecas, it will be remembered, had taken no part in Pontiac's war. The latter had now become disaffected toward the chief, and in this state of affairs, Sir William Johnson induced a number of the Iroquois warriors to march against his men, offering a reward of fifty dollars each for the heads of Onuperaquedra and Long Coat, the two principal Delaware chiefs. The party set out and in a few days came upon a camp of forty Delawares under Captain Bull, another noted chief, who were marching against the settlement. They rushed upon this camp during the night and took every one prisoner. They were conducted to Albany and thence to New York, where they were confined in the jail.

About this time, Johnson, then Superintendent of Indian affairs, and George Croghan, each addressed a memorial to the Lords of Trade, "setting forth the character, temper, and resources of the Indian tribes, and suggesting the course of conduct which they judged it expedient to pursue." This memorial stated the true causes of the disaffection of the different tribes to be the neglect and unjust treatment which they had received at the hands of the English. It suggested that, before resorting to arms, an attempt be made to conciliate them, to make them presents, to treat them with uniform kindness, to remove all causes of irritation, and, finally, to purchase a large tract of land, further westward to which the Indians should be induced to move, and where by wise government, their good-will might ever be retained.

This plan the British Government decided to adopt; but before doing so, it was evident to all that the conspiracy and the leading spirit of the tribes must be put down. No binding treaties could be made with the savages whose natures were so thoroughly brutalized and perfidious as Pontiac's coadjutors, and not until the tribes were made to feel they were *compelled* to respect their word, could any peace be hoped for. It was, therefore, determined to march two powerful armies into the Indian country. The first was to advance to Fort Pitt, and thence into the country of the Shawnees and Delawares; the second was to ascend the lakes and subdue the different tribes in the vicinity of Detroit. The last-named army was placed under the command of Colonel Bradstreet, a brave man, but, rash, short sighted and utterly disqualified for the important duty. The leader of the former was Colonel Bouquet, a Swiss, and First Lieutenant of the celebrated corps known as the Royal Americans. He combined in himself the qualities of kindness, judgment, absolute intrepidity, and was one of the best qualified leaders that ever did service in America. So skillful and self confident did he become in a few years, that it is said, in conducting his men through a dangerous passage in the forest, he often took a rifle and acted the part of advance scout. His kind treatment and regard for his men were such that the latter almost idolized him.

Colonel Bradstreet and his men (many of whom, in the language of Parkman, "looked more like candidates for a hospital than like men fit for the arduous duty before them," proceeded westward, up the Mohawk, through Oswego river and across Lake Ontario to Fort Niagara. Previous to this Sir William Johnson had sent Indian runners to the different tribes, warning them of the preparations which were being made against them, and advising all who wished to escape the blow to meet Bradstreet at Niagara and make peace with him. The Indians had suffered so much from the stoppage of the fur trade, and the failure of the expected assistance from the French, that vast numbers embraced the opportunity, and, upon Colonel Bradstreet's arrival, he found over two thousand warriors assembled to meet him. They included Ojibwas, Ottawas, Menomonies, Mississaugas, Caughnawagas, Sacs, Foxes, Winnebagoes and deputies from the Six Nations.

As Sir William Johnson was the only one empowered to make peace, he was present, ready to meet the numerous chiefs. Before doing so, he received an insulting message from the Delawares and Shawnees, saying out of *pity* for the *old women* (English) they would make peace.

Councils were held with each of the assembled tribes, separately, and were conducted by Johnson in such a manner as to prevent their uniting into any confederacy. Among them were an Ottawa band from Mackinaw, who, it will be recollected, rescued the survivors of that massacre from the Ojibwas. Johnson acknowledged their services with great pleasure, and admonishing that their true interests lay in preserving peace with the English, accorded to them liberty to open traffic with the traders who were already collecting— a favor that had been refused all other tribes. Besides this, he gave them a good quantity of clothing, and, when one of them, at the conclusion of the council, made a pathetic appeal for some ' rum to comfort them,' he did not refuse. Of course they were greatly pleased, and doubtless made the treaty with the best of faith.

Johnson having concluded his labors, left Fort Niagara on the sixth of August, and soon after Bradstreet moved up to Fort Schlosser, above Niagara Falls. At this point, they were joined by seven hundred Indians and Canadians. Among the former was the Henry spoken of in the preceding chapter.

While on the route to Presqu'Isle they were visited by a number of chiefs from the Delawares and Shawnees, who asked for peace in the name of their tribes. Bradstreet was aware of the insulting message these same tribes had sent Sir William Johnson, and should have distrusted their professions

He had received peremptory instructions to avoid any treaty or alliance with them, and to deal with them as their outrageous deeds merited. The officers also cautioned Bradstreet, but, in the face of all this he entered into a preliminary treaty, by which he bound himself not to offer any hostilities for the space of twenty five days, at the expiration of which the pretended deputies agreed to meet him at Sandusky, and deliver up all the prisoners in their possession.

Bradstreet, elated at his unexpected success, sent a messenger to Colonel Bouquet, his superior officer saying that he might withdraw his troops, as he had reduced the Delawares and Shawnees to submission. Bouquet treated this message with silent contempt and pursued his way onward.

The object of the chiefs making the treaty with Bradstreet, was simply to check his advance until it should be too late in the season to proceed further. The Delawares and Shawnees did not abate their murders and outrages along the frontier, even while these negotiations were pending. His conduct brought upon him the severe censure of Gage, his Commander in-Chief.

Still, confident that the aim of the two expeditions had been fully attained, Bradstreet made his way to Sandusky where he had been ordered to attack the Wyandots and Ottawas. But their promise to make a treaty with him, caused him to refrain from hostilities and he sent Captain Morris with several Canadians and Indians to Pontiac to exhort him also to make peace. In fact, Bradstreet seemed to have imbibed the idea that his name was so all potent that no chief would refuse his overtures. The reception that his messenger, Morris, received, served somewhat to dispel the notion. Pontiac, as mentioned, was haranguing the Indians along the Maumee river in the Illinois country. Up this stream for many miles, Morris ascended in a canoe, and, while at a considerable distance in the interior he was met by several hundred Indians who treated him with great roughness, although very friendly toward his companions. As he entered the camp, the first form he encountered was that of Pontiac himself, whose countenance was by no means prepossessing, just then. Morris's most eloquent efforts were met by the plunder of his whole party, who were only allowed a canoe in which to depart. Had the Ottawas not known that many of their relations were in the hands of the army at Detroit, the probabilities are that the whole party would have been massacred. At Fort Miami, Morris escaped assassination by the merest accident of remaining in the canoe while the savages were searching the woods for him. He was afterward taken prisoner by them, stripped naked and saved by the daring of an Indian boy—the nephew of Pontiac. Returning to the fort he received notice that several Shawnee chiefs were approaching, with the express purpose of killing him. Under these circumstances he took the advice of the Canadians and made an expeditious retreat to Sandusky whence he forwarded Bradstreet an account of his embassy.

In the mean time, Bradstreet had made his way to Detroit where he arrived on the twenty sixth of August. As his boats came to view round the bend in the river, the booming cannon, the frenzied shouts and hurrahs, the waving of hats and handkerchiefs told the joyous fact that the SIEGE OF DETROIT was now ended. For fifteen months had the garrison been beleagured by a merciless enemy, and there was occasion to rejoice. It was an inspiriting sight, the gayly uniformed soldiers filing through the streets to the strains of martial music, the red banners floating proudly above them, the glowing countenances of the officers and men as they saluted each other, while, on the opposite side of the river, the Wyandots were leaping, hooting and screeching like demons.

The garrison was immediately relieved, and the new arrived troops substituted in their stead. Bradstreet set about arranging his treaties with the surrounding tribes. On the seventh of September, 1764, he met in the open air, deputations from the Ottawas, Ojibwas, Pottawatomies, Sacs, Miamis, and Wyandots. He demanded that the Indians should become subjects of Great Britain before he could consent to peace. "Nothing," remarks Parkman, "could be more absurd and impolitic than this demand. This article of treaty, could its purport have been fully understood, might have kindled afresh the quarrel which it sought to extinguish but, happily, not a savage present was able to comprehend it. Subjection and sovereignty are ideas which never enter into the mind of an Indian, therefore his language has no words to express them." The treaty, however, was concluded, the deputies being in blissful ignorance of half its meaning.

Bradstreet most imprudently employed a French interpreter in his communications. This so incensed the Iroquois, who could not understand a word uttered, that they refused the ceremony of shaking hands, affirming that they had not heard the speeches, and, consequently, did not know whether they were dealing with friends or enemies. This was hardly noticed by Bradstreet, who returned to Sandusky to keep his promise with the Shawnee and Delaware deputies, boasting that he had completely subdued all the tribes. He waited several days beyond the appointed time at Sandusky, but no chiefs appeared. After a time several savages came into camp, and told him if he would remain quiet and not harm their villages, the prisoners would be forthcoming in a week. He readily consented, but, before that time was expired, received a stinging communication from Gage, ordering him to advance at once against the Indians. About the same time, he received Captain Morris's journals, and saw at once what an egregious dupe the Indians had made of him. His chagrin was so great that instead of obeying his Commander in Chief he affirmed that the march ordered could not be made; and, at length, struck his camp and returned to the settlements, where the levied troops disbanded and the regulars went into winter quarters.

This expedition, illy conducted as it was, produced its good results. The posts on the upper lakes were all re-established, and the siege of Detroit was ended. But, the wavering, imbecile course of Bradstreet so incensed the Iroquois under him, that, when they left him, they had imbibed the most thorough contempt for English arms, and not Sir William Johnson even was able to counteract their pernicious impression.

While the expedition was inactive, another was in progress under the admirable leadership of Colonel Bouquet. On the seventeenth of September he reached Fort Pitt with his men, and, while there, was waited upon by three pretended Delaware deputies in the same manner that Bradstreet had been visited. Instead of treating, he questioned them closely; and convinced that they were nothing more than spies, seized three One of them he sent home with a message saying, that, as the Delawares had violated their treaty with Colonel Bradstreet, he was marching against their towns with the intention of punishing them, but that, if they would give satisfaction for their outrages, he would be merciful and spare their families. He said that he had sent two messengers to Bradstreet, and if they were disturbed or injured, he would put both his prisoners to death and show the tribe no mercy.

This message had great effect upon the Indians. They saw they had to deal with a man who was not afraid to do his duty, and many began to advocate peace.

Before starting, several Iroquois spies visited Bouquet and endeavored to persuade him from attempting the expedition, assuring him that the way was so difficult they could never succeed, while, if he remained in his present quarters for a time, the Indians would soon bring in their prisoners and make an unconditional submission. This was only a ruse to retard his progress, as had been done with Bradstreet, but, not heeding their warnings, the commander sent them to the hostile tribes with a notice that he would soon be among them unless complete atonement was made.

In the early part of October, Colonel Bouquet entered a wilderness through which no army had ever marched. His progress was necessarily slow, encumbered by numbers of sheep, cattle, and their heavy equipage, but his men pressed cheerfully onward, and ten days after leaving the fort, they crossed the river Muskingum. He was now in the Indian country. The inhabitants were filled with the greatest terror at his approach. Passing down the Muskingum, he selected a beautiful camping ground, and ordered the chiefs to meet him in council. He appointed a place a short distance below the camp, which was strongly guarded by his men, to prevent treachery. At the appointed time a large number of chiefs, among whom were Custaloga of the Delawares, Kiashuta of the Senecas, and the head chief of the Shawnees whose name no living man can spell. The expression upon each of their faces was as black and threatening as the thunder cloud, and they seemed perfectly willing that their intense hatred of the English should be seen by all. After going through their usual ceremony of smoking, a Delaware addressed the council,

His speech was dignified and savoring somewhat of independence. At its close he delivered up eighteen prisoners, promising to do the same with all in their possession as soon as they could be collected. The council then adjourned, according to custom, to give Bouquet time to prepare his speech.

When the time arrived, he arose and made a *speech*. He didn't take time to call them fathers or brothers, but came to the point without any rhetorical circumlocution. He told them they had robbed and murdered their traders in time of peace, had attacked Fort Pitt which had been built by their consent, had assaulted and been defeated by his own troops at Bushy Run, had continually ravaged the frontier, and while one party was making peace with Colonel Bradstreet, another was murdering and scalping the defenseless settlers. He added that they had sent an insulting message to Sir William Johnson, had refused to make peace, and never kept any of their engagements. "You are all in our power," said Bouquet, "and if we choose we can exterminate you from the earth, but the English are a merciful people, averse to shed the blood even of their greatest enemies; and, if it were possible that you could convince us that you sincerely repent of your past perfidy, and that we could *depend* on your good behavior for the future, you might yet hope for mercy and peace." The speaker then informed them that he would give them twelve days to bring in every prisoner, English or French, married or unmarried, whether adopted or not; that all these should be furnished with clothing, provisions and horses to take them to Fort Pitt, and that, until all these conditions were complied with, he would consider them enemies, and receive no offers of peace.

This speech "told" with astonishing effect. All haughtiness and independence left the chiefs. When the council broke up they set about collecting their prisoners with great expedition. They saw at a glance that deception would prove their ruin. When the twelve days had expired, over two hundred captives were given up, and the stern, determined course of the leader had subdued the Delawares and Shawnees as completely as if he had destroyed all their villages and slain half their warriors. Colonel Bouquet saw this—he understood the Indian character. Now the spirit and very letter of his demands were complied with, he gave way to the natural kindness of his heart. He extended the hand of fellowship, and told them they were now brethren. He advised them to send deputies to Sir William Johnson, who would make treaties with them. This the Indians did, expressing, at the same time, the best of satisfaction with Bouquet's course. This was one of the greatest victories gained without the shedding of a drop of blood.

The troops now returned to Fort Pitt, where the recovered captives were restored to their homes, and the provincials disbanded, after receiving a handsome compliment from their beloved leader. The Pennsylvania Assembly, at its next session, passed a vote of thanks to Colonel Bouquet, referring to his services in the warmest terms. The Virginia Assembly did the same, and both recommended him to the king as worthy of promotion. His services, however, had been already recognized. He was appointed to the rank of Brigadier, and given command of the southern department. Here he won the love and respect of all by his many virtues, his nobleness of heart, and universal kindness. Three years later he was attacked with fever and died at Pensacola, and many an eye was moistened and many a heart was saddened when the mournful tidings was received, for he was "a gallant soldier and a generous man."

CHAPTER IX

THE CONSPIRATOR FOILED—HE BURIES THE HATCHET—HIS SUBSEQUENT LIFE AND DEATH—SUMMARY OF HIS CHARACTER

Deserted by his own people, refused assistance by the French—forced to fly by the approach of the hated English—where was Pontiac? Amid all this ruin, the proud chief rose like an untamed lion with the fires of his ambition still burning and still urging him on to new schemes and deeds.

From the river Maumee Pontiac, followed by several hundred of his warriors, went westward in the fall of 1764 into the country of the Kickapoos, Piankishaws and the

Miamis. Everywhere he stirred up the tribes by his resistless eloquence, he was kindling a conflagration more extensive—more disastrous in its consequences than any that yet had swept along the frontier. As soon as he saw the fire burning, he journeyed on to the Mississippi, where he met the Illinois in council, and compelled them to enlist under his standard. From here he proceeded to Fort Chartres, one of the principal French forts, and, after making a speech to the commandant, demanded arms, ammunition and troops. He was refused as kindly as the commandant could do it, but, enraged and still determined, Pontiac had a wampum belt of extraordinary size constructed, which he placed in the hands of a chosen few, with instructions to journey down the Mississippi and display it to the different tribes along the shores. These were to be urged to prevent any English passing up stream. The embassy were then to proceed to New Orleans, and demand assistance of the Governor.

The growing spirit of hostility among the different Indians was greatly increased by two occurrences that became known about this time. In the previous spring, Major Loftus commenced ascending the Mississippi with four hundred regulars, intending to take possession of Fort Chartres. When about two hundred and fifty miles above New Orleans, he was fired into by some concealed Indians, and a number of his men were slain. In the greatest terror, he retreated to New Orleans, whence he made his way to Pensacola.

A short time later, Captain Pittman arrived at New Orleans with the intention of ascending to the Illinois, but the reports of danger, and the solicitations of friends finally induced him to abandon his designs.

These repulses gave the Indians great confidence, and Pontiac's embassy found their work an easy task among them. They were greeted with yells of delight, and were only too ready to engage in the bloody work. Arriving at New Orleans, they found the place in a great tumult. The inhabitants had learned but a few weeks before, that France had ceded their town to Spain. A more detested proceeding could not have been inflicted by their Government, and the people were waiting in the momentary expectation of the hated change of masters.

D'Abbadie, the Governor, although on the very brink of the grave, received the embassy in his council house, and listened attentively to their message. He replied in a feeble and trembling voice, endeavoring to soothe their passions, and the council, according to established custom, adjourned until the next day. D'Abbadie died that night, and Aubry, his successor, received the envoys the next morning. After condoling with their white brother upon their misfortune, a Miami chief addressed a most cutting speech to the Governor, accusing his people of lying, and being whipped into submission by the English. He added that they were independent of the French, and only demanded the powder and arms they had used in their service. Aubry, making a few presents, endeavored to conciliate them; but, when the embassy turned their faces again up the Mississippi, a deeper hatred than ever rankled in their hearts.

General Gage, the Commander in Chief, was now convinced that there was no prospect of peace so long as the flag of France floated over a single post in the ceded territory; for the Indians still cherished the hope of her assistance, and would continue so to do as long as she held the least semblance of power. The great danger of attempting to ascend the Mississippi, induced Gage to form a determination to march an army by the way of the Ohio, the success of Bouquet having cleared this route. Before doing this, however, Sir William Johnson dispatched his deputy, George Croghan, with the object of distributing presents, of arguing the matter with them, and, if possible, to disabuse their minds of their prejudices against the English.

Croghan and his companion set out in February 1765. After journeying hundreds of miles through all the perils of the wilderness, they reached Fort Pitt, where they waited for the train to come up. This, however, was attacked and completely robbed by the notorious "Paxton men," so that Croghan was deprived of one of his most powerful auxiliaries. Replacing his loss as well as he could from Fort Pitt, he sent his assistant forward to the Illinois, while he remained to hold council with the Delawares and Shawnees, which they had promised their conqueror Bouquet the year before.

Lieutenant Frazer took leave of Croghan with several

companions, journeyed a thousand miles down the Mississippi, into the country of the Illinois, where, as Parkman remarks, "he found himself in a nest of hornets." So great, indeed, was his danger, that he made a precipitate retreat in disguise to New Orleans.

Croghan having concluded his treaties at Fort Pitt, left that place in May, and, attended by several Shawnee and Delaware chiefs, descended the Ohio. Just as they had landed, near the mouth of the Wabash, they were attacked by nearly a hundred Kickapoos, several of the party killed, and all made prisoners; not, however, until three of the assailing Indians had fallen.

This attack of the Kickapoos appears to have been merely one of those outbreaks peculiar to the Indian character—the gratification of a whim, without a thought of the consequences. When they became sensible of what they had really done they were sorely frightened, and begged forgiveness like so many children, declaring that they believed the Indians in the party to be Cherokees, their implacable enemies. Still retaining the party as prisoners, the Kickapoos made their way to Vincennes where the captives were warmly greeted and the captors as warmly reproved for what they had done. They next proceeded to Ouatanon where Croghan made his quarters in the fort.

Here he commenced business. Tribe after tribe sent its deputies in, and the council-house, for several days, may be said to have been wrapped in a fog, on account of the continual calumets that were smoking. This, with the ceremonious speeches and the shaking of hands, formed the routine of each day's business. Affairs could not have progressed more favorably. The Indians seemed to be swayed by reason instead of passion, and Croghan fondly believed the sun of peace was already rising in the sky.

Warrior after warrior had left Pontiac, until he was nearly deserted. All was lost. To hold out longer would be destruction, to fly was scarcely an easier task. In the south lay the Cherokees, hereditary enemies of his people. In the west were the Osages and Missouris, treacherous and uncertain friends, and the fierce and jealous Dahcotah. In the east the forests would soon be filled with English traders, and beset with English troops, while in the north his own village of Detroit lay beneath the guns of the victorious garrison. He might, indeed, have found a partial refuge in the remoter wilderness of the upper lakes, but those dreary wastes would have doomed him to a life of unambitious exile. His resolution was taken. He determined to accept the peace which he knew would be proffered, to smoke the calumet with his triumphant enemies, and patiently await his hour of vengeance."*

It must have cost the old monarch a mighty struggle to bring himself to this resolution—to yield all his ambitious dreams of greatness. He could but see that the inevitable doom of his race was already written, and, although the encroachment of the whites might be opposed, it never could be effectually stayed. Westward, through the coming ages, the tide of civilization must advance until it had reached that far off ocean which formed the western boundary of America, and until the last remnant of the aborigines had passed from the face of the earth.

From Ouatanon, Croghan journeyed toward Fort Chartres. He had gone but a short distance, when he met Pontiac, and a number of chiefs and warriors. Croghan's hand was taken by the fallen chief and all returned to the fort. Assembled in council, Pontiac made the usual overtures of peace, and uttered the most friendly feelings toward the English. He said the lies of the French had driven him to arms, but, now that their falsehoods were discovered, he would no longer oppose the English; yet, at the same time he assured Croghan that the French did not own the land, and therefore had no right to sell it. It still belonged to his own people. As a pledge of Pontiac's sincerity, he accompanied Croghan on his return to Detroit, attending, with his chiefs, all the councils which were held along the Maumee.

Detroit was reached in August, 1765, where Croghan summoned the different tribes to meet him for the purpose of establishing treaties, and adjusting difficulties. They answered his call with great readiness, for they saw their own interest lay in obtaining the good will of those who had conquered both the Indians and French. All those who had

* Tallman.

been hostile made their appearance, even the chief who had been the prime mover and leader in the massacre at Mackinaw. He expressed great sorrow for what he had done, and humbly asked for peace.

Some days later Croghan met the Ottawas in council, and addressed them in the following high wrought style:

"Children, we are very glad to see so many of you here present at your ancient council fire, which has been neglected for some time past, since then, high winds have blown, and raised heavy clouds over your country. I now, by this belt, rekindle your ancient fire, and throw dry wood upon it, that the blaze may ascend to heaven, so that all nations may see it, and know that you live in peace and tranquillity with your fathers the English.

"By this belt I disperse all the black clouds from over your heads, that the sun may shine clear on your women and children, that those unborn may enjoy the blessing of this general peace, now so happily settled between your father the English and you and all your younger brethren to the sunsetting.

"Children, by this belt I gather up all the bones of your deceased friends, and bury them deep in the ground, that the buds and sweet flowers of the earth may grow over them, that we may not see them any more.

"Children, with this belt I take the hatchet out of your hand, and pluck up a large tree, and bury it deep, so that it may never be found any more; and I plant the tree of peace, which all our children may sit under, and smoke in peace with their fathers.

"Children, we have made a road from the sunrising to the sun-setting. I desire that you will preserve that road good and pleasant to travel upon, that we may all share the blessings of this happy union."

The council reassembled on the next day, and Pontiac, representative of the different tribes, replied to Croghan as follows:

"Father, we have all smoked out of this pipe of peace. It is your children's pipe; and as the war is all over, and the Great Spirit and Giver of Light, who has made the earth and every thing therein, has brought us all together this day for our mutual good, I declare to all nations that I have settled my peace with you before I came here, and now deliver my pipe to be sent to Sir William Johnson, that he may know I have made peace, and taken the King of England for my father, in presence of all the nations now assembled, and whenever any of those nations go to visit him, they may smoke out of it with him in peace. Fathers, we are obliged to you for lighting up our old council-fire for us, and desiring us to return to it, but we are now settled on the Miami river, not far from hence; whenever you want us, you will find us there."

Croghan having fully accomplished all for which he had been sent, now returned to Niagara, Pontiac promising to accept an invitation to visit Oswego the next spring and conclude a treaty with Sir William Johnson himself. The winter passed away without any incident of note, and Pontiac, with a number of his chiefs redeemed his promise made to Croghan. Through Lake Erie and Ontario the little company passed, and were greeted with the booming of cannon from the Oswego batteries as it reached its destination. Here Sir William Johnson with a number of Iroquois, was waiting to receive them; and, on the twenty-third of July, the vast assembly was convened in open air. The preliminary ceremonies occupied all of the first day; but upon the second Sir William Johnson addressed himself to Pontiac and his companions: —

"Children, I bid you hearty welcome to this place, and I trust that the Great Spirit will permit us often to meet together in friendship, for I have now opened the door and cleared the road that all nations may come hither from the sunsetting. This belt of wampum confirms my words.

"Children, it gave me much pleasure to find that you who are present behaved so well last year and treated in so friendly a manner Mr Croghan, one of my deputies, and that you expressed such concern for the bad behavior of those, who, in order to obstruct the good works of peace, assaulted and wounded him and killed some of his party, both whites and Indians—a thing before unknown, and contrary to the laws and customs of all nations. This would have drawn down our strongest resentment upon those who were guilty of so heinous a crime, were it not for the great lenity and kindness of your English father, who does not delight in punishing those who repent sincerely of their faults.

"Children, I have now with the approbation of General Gage, (your father's chief warrior in this country,) invited you here in order to confirm and strengthen your proceedings with Mr. Croghan last year. I hope that you will remember all that then passed, and I desire that you will often repeat it, and keep it fresh in your minds.

"Children, you begin already to see the fruits of peace from the number of traders and plenty of goods at all the garrisoned posts, and our enjoying the peaceable possession of the Illinois will be found of great advantage to the Indians in that country. You likewise see that proper officers, men of honor and probity, are appointed to reside at the posts, to prevent abuses in trade, to hear your complaints, and to lay before me such of them as they can not redress. Interpreters are likewise sent for the assistance of each of them, and smiths are sent to the posts to repair your arms and implements. All this, which is attended with great expense, is now done by the great king, your father, as a proof of his regard, so that, casting from you all jealousy and apprehension, you should now strive with each other who should show the most gratitude to this best of princes. I do now, therefore, confirm the assurances which I give you of his majesty's good-will and do insist on your casting away all evil thoughts and shutting your ears against all flying idle reports of bad people."

In this strain, Johnson continued his speech, urging the Indians to give no credence to the numerous reports and falsehoods that would be circulated in and about them. On the next day, Pontiac replied, saying as he presented the belt of wampum —

"Father, when you address me, it is the same as if you addressed all the nations of the West. Father, this belt is to cover and strengthen our chain of friendship, and to show you that, if any nation shall lift the hatchet against our English brethren, we shall be the first to feel it and resent it."

Thus closed this memorable council. Pontiac once more

proceeded to the Maumee, where he had made his home, and carrying with him, we may believe, a sincere determination to abide by the treaty which he had made. There are strong grounds for this in the fact, that in a short time some trouble sprung up along the frontier, which grew into a war on the Virginia border, yet Pontiac took no part in it. His name is never once mentioned in the records of these times, and the probabilities are that he employed himself, as did the Indians around him, in hunting, fishing and the sports of the chase.

For the period of several years all trace is lost of him. In 1769 he made his appearance among the Illinois, where he excited much apprehension among the English in that section. He remained but a short time, when he went to St. Louis and visited a house, of which Pierre Chouteau was an inmate.* He also called upon several others, all of whom received him with the greatest cordiality.

A few days later Pontiac remarked that he should cross to Cahokia upon the opposite side of the river, where a number of Indians were holding a sort of drunken frolic. His friends sought to dissuade him, as they believed his life would be endangered; but, self confident as of old, he was afraid of no one, and crossed with several of his companions in a canoe. He found the village swarming with Illinois Indians and Creoles, and was soon invited to a great feast. Here the bottle passed freely and Pontiac became deeply intoxicated. When the feast was finished, he arose and went pitching, swaggering and singing down the street, and wandered off into the woods.

He had scarcely entered the forest when a Kaskaskia Indian —who had been bribed to the deed by an English trader—stole noiselessly after him, and followed his footsteps with a tread as stealthy as the panther's. While the chief was still chanting the medicine song and strolling aimlessly forward, the keen tomahawk clove his skull in twain, and his corpse dropped heavily to the earth.

In a short time, the dead body was discovered, and the

---

* This Pierre Chouteau was still living in 1846 and was visited by Mr. Parkman at his country seat near St. Louis. He entertained a distinct remembrance of the chief and of all the circumstances of his visit. Pontiac was arrayed in the dress of a French officer which had been presented to him by Montcalm during the French war.

wildest yells announced the event. Pontiac's followers scattered to the different villages, and the news spread like wild fire; hatchets were snatched up; chiefs, sachems and warriors of different tribes made the cause common, and hundreds, thirsting for revenge, descended upon the Illinois tribes.

The death of Pontiac was most fearfully avenged. Whole tribes were exterminated. The Peorias, Kaskaskias, and Cahokias were nearly or quite exterminated, and, as his historian remarks, "over the grave of Pontiac more blood was poured out in atonement than flowed from the hecatombs of slaughtered heroes on the corpse of Patroclus."

Thus died the great Conspirator. He was a man shrewd, cunning and treacherous, with a masterly and far-seeing mind; one who embodied within himself all the virtues and many of the vices of his people; a man of towering ambition and wonderful genius—whose influence over the wayward passions of his race was absolute and supreme. His life, like his death, is written in blood.

A half century later the spirit of the dead Conspirator seemed to spring into being again, and to go forth through fields of slaughter in the guise of the Shawnee chief, TECUMSEH—so alike were the twain in courage, in sagacity, in ambition and ferocity toward the white race.

May the world never see his like again!

CPSIA information can be obtained
at www.ICGtesting.com
Printed in the USA
LVHW111949230122
709154LV00008B/1027